1 PETER
God's Chosen People

Let the word of Christ dwell in you richly as you teach and admonish
one another with all wisdom, and as you sing psalms, hymns and spiritual
songs with gratitude in your hearts to God (Colossians 3:16).

D0034332

By Martin H. Scharlemann
Prepared by Debb Andrus
Edited by Rodney L. Rathmann

CPH™
SAINT LOUIS

Contents

Leaders Notes

Lesson 1

The Message of an Apostle (Overview)

Our Goal Today

Our goal in this lesson is that we may acquire an overall grasp of **1 Peter** as an apostolic document and, therefore, as authoritative for every generation of readers and hearers.

Introductory Points

Many ancient secular documents are lost to us. Some of the finest were destroyed when famous libraries, such as those at Alexandria in ancient Egypt, burned. Yet God, in His providence, preserved for His church those books that we speak of as "the prophetic and apostolic Word." **1 Peter** offers such an apostolic message. Hence we do not read it like a work from Plato, who was not an apostle. We study this epistle as material that addresses us directly through the working of the Holy Spirit, bringing us to faith in Jesus Christ or enriching the faith in which we already live by Baptism.

The Salutation

In the days of the apostle Peter people wrote letters in a way somewhat different from our modern-day practices. It was customary for the writer to name himself first and then to indicate to whom he was writing. These two items were followed by a greeting—and sometimes also a prayer-wish or even a thanksgiving.

Identify these three parts of a salutation in **Acts 23:26; James 1:1;** and then in **1 Peter 1:1–2.**

The Author

In this epistle the author used the name that Jesus gave him (see **Matthew 16:18** and **John 1:42**). At home he had been known as Simon, the son of John (bar-Jonah). As an apostle, however, he preferred to be called Peter (Cephas), the rock man. He had, with his confession of faith, been chosen and created as the person whose name would head the list of the Twelve and so mark the beginning of the new Israel, just as Abraham had been selected to be the rock from which Israel of old had been hewn (see **Isaiah 51:1–2**).

The Recipients and the Greeting

After naming himself, Peter described himself as an apostle of Jesus Christ and then went on to describe the first recipients of this letter. Then, instead of the usual "greetings," the apostle wrote, "Grace and peace be yours in abundance" **(v. 2)**. Here he followed a pattern established by the Jewish High Council in Jerusalem. When this body of men wrote to a synagogue, they concluded their salutation with the words, "May peace be multiplied to you." Peter added the New Testament word *grace* in his salutation to fellow Christians in Asia Minor.

The Conclusion

From the salutation we move, for a brief moment, to the conclusion of this epistle **(5:12–14)**. There we note the mention of Silas (Silvanus) as the person who delivered the apostle's letter to the churches mentioned in the salutation. Some authorities believe that Silas may have served as Peter's scribe in the same sense that Tertius and Tychicus related to Paul (see **Romans 16:22** and **Ephesians 6:21**). The concluding verses state the purposes of the epistle and include greetings. The last sentence comprises a wish for peace, or, as a Jewish person like Peter would say, "Shalom!"

The Body

Between the salutation and conclusion, of course, is the body of the letter. Its wording indicates that the apostle was writing mainly to persons who either had just been baptized or were about to take part in this sacrament. In essence, Peter was addressing himself to the question that every new convert had, and still has, to ask: Is it really worthwhile to be a Christian?

At **4:11** Peter breaks into a doxology. Some commentators suggest that the first part of the epistle, either up to **4:6** or **4:11,** is a baptismal homily directed to newly baptized people, followed by more general words of exhortation and direction to the congregations as a whole. We might, therefore, liken the first part to a confirmation sermon. The unity of the document is not affected by calling attention to these two major sections. It would help to account for the liturgical quality of the main body of the letter.

The Sequence

Epistles were not written to be outlined. Yet, as a rule, determining movements in the author's thinking will help the reader understand more fully the individual passages of an epistle.

There are, roughly speaking, three doctrinal sections, each one of which is followed by some ethical applications:

1 Peter 1:3–12: What the triune God has done for our salvation (doctrine)

1 Peter 1:13–25: The kind of lifestyle that such action on God's part calls for (ethics)

1 Peter 2:1–10: The means of grace at work in the priesthood of believers (doctrine)

1 Peter 2:11–3:17: Living to the glory of God (ethics); this section includes what we call a table of duties **(2:13–3:12)**

1 Peter 3:18–22: How Christ established His lordship over the total universe (doctrine)

1 Peter 4:1–5:11: The new way of life in response to the awareness that "the end of all things is near" (ethics)

The very fact that the apostle puts doctrine before ethics points out the proper sequence in which God works for our salvation. He acts first; then He moves us to respond to His gracious approach. This is the exact reverse of what every religion except Christianity teaches. In Jesus' day, for example, rabbis said, "Repent; then God's kingdom will come." Both John the Baptist and Jesus proclaimed, "Repent; for the kingdom of God has come to you" (see **Matthew 3:2** and **Mark 1:15**).

The Occasion

Commentaries suggest various dates for the writing of this epistle, all the way from A.D. 63 to A.D. 112. Anyone who argues for a date beyond the sixties of the first century thereby implies that the epistle was not really written by Simon Peter. Yet the letter explicitly claims to have been written by him.

Peter did not date the letter. Therefore we must try to derive our conclusions from internal evidence. Two things stand out very clearly: (1) the people to whom the apostle was writing were suffering some kind of social harassment (see **4:12; 3:14; 1:6**); and (2) they were new converts and were being received into the church or had just become members (see **1:22**). The members of the congregations named in the salutation were shaken up by what they were experiencing, wondering whether God's children should really be expected to stand for suffering (see **2:21–23**).

When may this have happened? It probably took place in connection with the persecution of the Christians following the burning of Rome in A.D. 64. Peter probably wrote this epistle from Rome, which the early Christians often referred to as Babylon (see **5:13**). He dispatched the epistle by Silas to the churches in Pontus, etc., **(v. 1)**, to reassure them in their puzzlement and distress. Shortly after writing this letter of comfort, Peter was crucified.

The Destination

The opening verses of **1 Peter** clearly indicate to what areas this letter was first sent. Judging from the sequence in which the provinces are listed, Silas (and others who may have accompanied him) probably left Rome by ship and landed at Sinope, the main port of the Roman province of Pontus (on the northern coast of what is today Turkey). Then he moved by way of Galatia and Cappadocia westward to Asia (of which Ephesus was the capital) and from there northward to Bithynia, which at that time was part of Pontus. From there it was possible to return to Rome, if that is what he chose to do. (We are not told.)

The Purpose

1 Peter has a twofold purpose, as indicated in the conclusion **(5:12)**: (1) to offer consolation and encouragement; and (2) to add the apostle's personal testimony to the truth of God's grace and, therefore, of the church's proclamation. On the basis of these stated purposes, Peter asks his readers to stand fast.

Authority

The second purpose underlines this letter's authority. In **5:12** Peter adds to his own personal witness. He does so as an apostle of Jesus Christ **(1:1)**. That makes **1 Peter** an apostolic document. Hence its message is binding for all time on those who confess their faith in the one, holy, Christian (catholic), and apostolic church.

For Group Discussion

1. What do you recall about Peter the person and Peter the Christian that will help you read and understand better his first letter?

2. How would you compare yourself with the people who first read this letter?

3. In your own words summarize Peter's purpose for writing this letter **(5:12).**

A Glimpse Ahead

From these considerations about the origins, structure, and purpose of **1 Peter** we move forward to the text itself. In the next session we shall begin with a close analysis of the salutation **(1:1–2)** under the general title "There Is Nothing Like It" (the church).

Lesson 2

There Is Nothing Like It
(1 Peter 1:1–2)

Our Goal Today

Our goal in this lesson is that we may be moved by the apostle's word to appreciate more fully the size of God's grace as shown by His choosing us, before history ever began, as members of the New Israel, which is the church as God's own people in a very special sense.

Origin

According to these verses (1:1–2) what is the church? Perhaps it would be better to ask, *who* is the church? What makes the church, your congregation, different from such organizations as the Rotarians, the Kiwanis, Civitans, Optimists, etc.?

The church exists because God the Father drew up a blueprint for it long before history ever began.

It is one thing to draw up a blueprint; it is quite another to work it out. The latter task is the responsibility of the Holy Spirit, as the text indicates. He has been given the assignment called *sanctification*. What does that word mean? The Bible teaches that the Holy Spirit not only calls us by the Gospel, He also enlightens us with His gifts and sanctifies us. What this means is that the third person of the Trinity implements God the Father's choice of us, which was made way back in eternity. In this way the church, as the assembly of believers, is created and is present right here, in this place, where we gather around Word and Sacrament.

Background

While, in a sense, the church is part of the "new" in the New Testament age, going back particularly to the first Pentecost **(Acts 2),** it has as its background the whole story of God's dealings with His people during the days of the Old Testament. To remind us of this fact, the apostle applies to us three words which, in the Old Testament, are used in reference to Israel. They are the words *elect, strangers* (i.e., resident aliens), and *scattered.* Compare the words used in other versions.

All three concepts are used by the apostle to remind us that the church, as the new Israel, stands in succession to God's ancient people. Thus we have a long history behind us. Our story goes back all the way to creation and to the fall of humankind. In particular, however, the story of the church has its roots in God's gracious choice of Israel **(Deuteronomy 7:6–8)** as His people, which, for much of its history, has lived in dispersion because of sin (see **Deuteronomy 4:27**). Hence, Israel of old, like Abraham, may properly be described as "a stranger" and "an alien" (see **Psalm 39:12**).

We must ask ourselves how these words describe us who belong to the church as the new Israel. In what sense are we modern-day Christians "aliens" like Abraham or Israel of old?

Purpose

The triune God created the church to serve a particular purpose. That purpose is indicated in the words, "for obedience to Jesus Christ and sprinkling by His blood." This phrase is best understood in light of what we are told in **Exodus 24:3–8.** Which words in this **Exodus** passage spell out the meaning of *covenant?* It is important to note in what way and for what purpose God made Israel His covenant nation, because those very ideas are applied by the apostle to us of the church.

Where does the word *covenant* occur in our worship service? (Your church may use the word *testament* in place of *covenant,* but the meaning is the same.)

How is it connected there with blood, the blood of Jesus Christ?

With the **Exodus** reference in mind it is not difficult to see how the expression "sprinkled by His blood" applies to us. By Jesus' death a new covenant was established once and for all. This part of our redemption was assigned to the second person of the Trinity: to seal our very special relationship to God by the shedding of His blood.

Means

Compare the way a civic club (such as the Rotatary or Kiwanis) gets its work done with the manner in which the church goes about her work. What similarities can you think of? What differences are there?

It may be helpful here to have a quick look at the words church fathers have used to describe the church: "The church is the assembly of saints in which the Gospel is taught purely and the sacraments are administered rightly." Of this group of people Jesus declared that the very "gates of Hades" shall not prevail against it **(Matthew 16:18).** Only God in His grace could have thought of such simple means for carrying on His work of salvation. The means of grace bear the same power that once called into being the world itself (see **2 Corinthians 4:6**). In this way the church is unique.

During the reformation period, as well as at other times, some people and congregations were infected with what has been called "enthusiasm." That is to say, they turned their own feelings and their prayers into means of grace. Have you noticed any symptoms of this happening in the church of today?

What role does God desire prayer to play in the life of a Christian?

Why is it risky to trust one's own feelings as the final judge in matters pertaining to God?

The church has been entrusted with the apostolic Word. It is in this gathering of God's people that His grace and peace are at work. Both are "in abundance" to meet whatever needs arise to trouble God's people. Accordingly, Peter closed his salutation with the wish that this may continue to happen: that God's undeserved favor (grace) as well as the calm and splendor of the Messianic age (peace) may increase more and more. At the very outset of this epistle Peter, therefore, reminds us that he was writing as an apostle of Jesus Christ.

For Group Discussion

1. Some have likened churches to drug stores: they are places you go to when you need help badly. Comment.

2. Name a number of great nations in history that have perished since the days of the apostle, while the church continues her work amid the debris of history.

3. What do we mean when we say in the Nicene Creed, "I believe in one holy Christian and apostolic Church?"

4. What is the relationship between the general word *church* and *congregation?*

A Glimpse Ahead

Next time we will consider our destiny as Christians.

Lesson 3

A People with a Place to Go (1 Peter 1:3–9)

Our Goal Today

Our goal in this lesson is that we may be given a deeper insight into the nature of our status as pilgrim people on our way to a destiny secured for us by our gracious God.

God Acted in Mercy

The note of us being pilgrim people was sounded already in Peter's salutation. The word there that was translated as *strangers* (NIV, NET, KJV) or *exiles* (RSV) contains also the thought of a people going somewhere, just as the Israelites were pilgrims in the desert on their way to the Promised Land.

We are on our way and not here to stay. We share in that privileged status by virtue of God's "great mercy" **(v. 3)**. There was and is nothing half-hearted or stingy about God's love. It abounds so that our cup runs over (see **Psalm 23:5**).

We must note how the apostle phrased his opening statement. The sentence reads like a thanksgiving: "Praise be . . ." The salutations of ancient letters were at times followed by just such a prayer-thought. In this case the wording follows that of the form of a Jewish blessing. We would normally say, "Thanks be to God!" But Peter had grown up as a Jew. From childhood on, therefore, he learned to give praise to God.

What items are given in **verse 3** that no Jew could or would confess? By this time, remember, Peter was a Christian, confessing Jesus Christ as his Lord, and God as the Father of that Lord Jesus Christ. That God—the only one there is!—had acted out of the abundance of His mercy to turn life around, so to speak, by arranging for our rebirth.

Baptism: Means of New Birth

How did God accomplish all this? "Through the resurrection of Jesus Christ from the dead." With that act of power God arranged to have all people declared to be righteous because of the obedience of one person, the Christ incarnate (see **Romans 5:19–21**). But, of course, that radically new relationship with God would not be of much benefit to us if there were no way of appropriating it to us individually. The benefits of Jesus Christ's resurrection become ours when we are (or were) baptized. That is what this reference to new birth means. By the Sacrament of Baptism we are taken up into the company of God; for it is that means of grace by which faith is created in us. Can you name the date of your own Baptism? In one way that is as important to know as your birthday.

Our Promised Land

The turnabout that has taken place by way of Jesus' resurrection and our Baptism is so great that life has taken on new meaning. We have been born anew to hope. Can you find two other words for "hope" in **verses 4 and 5?**

Read **Ephesians 2:12** to see what the apostle Paul says there on the subject of hope.

People in ancient times believed that history and life itself went round in a circle. Neither had a particular purpose or meaning. Into that kind of hopeless existence the Gospel burst with its message that God was active in history, having changed everything around by raising Jesus from the dead and thereby offering all people His grace by way of Baptism.

To such living hope we have been born again. Even death has been overcome. It has, in fact, become the entrance way to eternal life. Look up

1 Corinthians 15:23–28 to see the connection.

Three major concepts about the future comprise the heart of **verses 3–6.** They are *hope, inheritance,* and *salvation.* All three derived from ancient Israel's relationship to God as the Lord of history.

Behind the word *hope* is an Old Testament term that means "trust" and is applied to confidence in God for the future on the basis of what He promised and delivered in the past (see **Jeremiah 29:11**). In short, *hope,* as used by the apostle, is not the effervescent outlook expressed in the musical *South Pacific,* which speaks of "being stuck like a dope with a thing called hope." When **1 Peter** is referred to as "the epistle of hope," that means it deals with a relationship we have to God in faith—a faith turned to the future!

Inheritance, too, is a word about the future. It is applied in the Old Testament to Canaan as Israel's Promised Land. The apostle uses the term in **verse 4;** but then he goes on to describe the inheritance we are looking forward to as being unlike ancient Canaan since ours is imperishable, undefiled, and unfading because it is "kept in heaven." How do these three adjectives apply to our heavenly inheritance?

The word translated as *kept* really means "on deposit." It assures us that our eternal destiny is waiting for us. Since it is kept in heaven for us, it is not subject to the destruction of warfare (imperishable), the stain of idolatry (undefiled), and the ravages of time (unfading).

There is a third term we must consider, namely, *salvation* **(v. 5).** While, of course, our own salvation has its source in God's past actions, the concept has a future sense. Everything needed for our being set free, says the apostle, is ready to be revealed at the last moment. No essential element of our salvation is missing. What we await is the striking of the hour. Then we shall see and experience it fully. In short, *salvation* also has a future thrust because it is rooted in God's actions of the past. This is another way of saying that as members of the church, baptized in the name of the triune God, we live with the constant tension contained in the formula: already-not yet!

Share an experience from your own life that has revealed the tension expressed in the formula "already-not yet."

Shielded by God's Power

Even though our salvation is kept for us in heaven, we need God's attending strength to guard us on the way. By faith Jesus Christ, our Savior, has made us the benefactors of His protective power. Can you cite instances of this power at work to shield and protect you and your faith?

Such protection does not exempt any Christian from possible suffering and harassment. After all, our Lord suffered not with a view to have us escape difficulties but to provide the opportunity for us to share in His suffering (see **Philippians 3:10**). As a matter of fact, Peter makes the point that being subjected to various trials is a refining process like that of putting gold to the fire for purposes of burning away the dross.

The end product of such suffering is the kind of genuine faith that responds to God in lives that offer praise, honor, and glory to Him.

A Joy That Defies Definition

The verb *rejoice* occurs two times in **verses 6–9.** It points to the remarkable fact that Christians can go on their way rejoicing in the face of all disappointments and distress. Here you have one of the hallmarks of the Christian life. Read **Acts 5:41** to see why the apostles rejoiced as they left a session of the Sanhedrin (the Jewish high court), which had been arranged for the sole purpose of harassing and persecuting them. Why does such joy defy definition?

Peter, of course, had personally seen Jesus with his own eyes. His readers had not. Yet Peter described his readers as loving their Lord, believing in Him, and rejoicing in the final outcome of their faith, namely, the salvation of their souls. In what way are we in the same situation as the first readers of this epistle?

For Group Discussion

1. Discuss different meanings of the word *hope*.

2. The church has often been accused of preaching "pie in the sky, by and by." Comment.

3. It has been said that the problem that haunts people most today is that of meaninglessness. Do you agree?

4. Mention some of the mighty acts of God as related in the Old Testament to show how He keeps His promises.

A Glimpse Ahead

The apostle has not yet completed his description of what God did to offer us a living hope. The next three verses (1 Peter 1:10–12) underline the privileges of our present status as God's new Israel, the church.

Lesson 4

Our Present Privilege
(1 Peter 1:10–12)

Our Goal Today

Our goal in this lesson is that we may be led to become more aware of the splendor surrounding every moment of our gathering around God's Word and Sacrament.

Salvation Foretold

The world was quite old already in Peter's day. Many nations had by then been dropped into the dustbin of history. All kinds of religions had made their respective claims. In a very real sense, the salvation proclaimed by God's messengers was radically new. These facts might lead critics and enemies of the Christian movement to argue, "The Gospel you teach can hardly be true since it is of such recent origin."

To this point the apostle addresses himself in today's Scripture verses. In an indirect way, therefore, he is responding to a very practical question that has often troubled recent converts or potential church members: Is it worthwhile to become a part of this movement? Have you yourself, perhaps, asked that question? If so, today's passage will prove helpful.

Can you tell from the text (v. 11) what was puzzling the prophets in particular? And just what was it that the Spirit of Christ at work in the prophets of old foretold as He pointed forward to the age of the Messiah?

What does the expression "Spirit of Christ" suggest as to the relationship among the three persons in the Godhead?

Both "sufferings" and "glories" **(v. 11)** occur in the plural. The sequence is important also for Christian living: the cross always comes before Easter. The crosses we bear, the sufferings we endure, comprise the prelude to the glory yet to be revealed in us (see **Romans 8:18**). Such an insight was bound to sustain the readers to whom Peter first wrote his letter. It is also a source of strength for us.

Fuller Dimensions

Prophets of old, we read, handled the sacred things of God, but they did not live to see the fulfillment of their expectations **(v. 12)**. In fact, they were specifically informed that the mysteries with which they were working were not to receive clarification until later. In short, over the life and work of Old Testament prophets God spoke a solemn, "Not yet!" Daniel, for example, was specifically told that "The words are closed up and sealed until the time of the end" **(Daniel 12:9)**. Here look at Jesus' own words along this line as given in **Matthew 13:17** and **Luke 10:24**.

There is a very important *now* in **verse 12**. It has all the emphasis put on it also in **John 13:31** and **Ephesians 3:5.** Examine these passages to see how they suggest that time itself is properly divided between B.C. and A.D. The fuller dimensions of God's revelation came with the life and ministry of Jesus Christ and the sending of the Holy Spirit.

The phrase in **verse 12** describing the Holy Spirit as "sent from heaven" is most certainly a reference to Pentecost. How many of the provinces mentioned in **1 Peter 1:1** are also named in **Acts 2:9?**

Your answer will show that persons from the regions to which Peter addressed his letter were present in Jerusalem on the day when God chose to "pour out [His] Spirit on all people" **(Acts 2:17)**. These individuals went back home after the miracle of Pentecost to proclaim what they had heard and seen.

Proclamation of the Gospel

While, of course, the Good News of fulfillment in Jesus Christ burst upon the world of Peter's day as something radically different, that Gospel found its beginnings and roots in the utterances and activities of prophets who had lived long ago. Peter was inspired to make this point because the message of Jesus Christ was being brought not only to fellow Jews but to Gentiles. Many Gentiles tended to believe that nothing could possibly reach further back into history than the story of the founding of Rome. To such people the apostle was saying very plainly, "The Gospel you are hearing from people who were in Jerusalem has a much longer history: it is rooted in God's foreknowledge **(v. 2)** and was foreshadowed by prophets throughout many long centuries before the coming of Jesus Christ."

Angelic Excitement

The circumstances of the church and the progress of its redemptive work excite the rapt attention of the very angels of God **(v. 12)**, for they have not experienced that kind of redemption. They can only marvel at what God has done and continues to do for and with us.

The apostle used the same word for the angels' "long to look" as that found in **Luke 24:12** and **John 20:5–11** of the disciples taking a peek into the empty tomb of Easter. This thought moved Charles Wesley to write these lines for one of his many hymns:

> The first-born sons of light
> Desire in vain its depths to see.
> They cannot reach the mystery:
> The length and breadth and height.

With these words in mind, what do you think great artists like Raphael and Botticelli were trying to say when they painted little angels hovering low over various baptismal scenes?

For Group Discussion

1. What do **verses 10–11** say to the matter of the inspiration of Scripture?

2. In what way did the pouring out of the Holy Spirit on Pentecost differ from His operations in the Old Testament?

3. What is the consequence for us that Gentiles had (have) the Gospel proclaimed to them?

A Glimpse Ahead

In our discussions so far we have been overwhelmed to read and hear of all that God has done for us. Therefore, next time we will begin a consideration of our life as response to God's actions on our behalf.

Lesson 5

Life as Response to God's Action (1 Peter 1:13–21)

Our Goal Today

Our goal in this lesson is that we may be guided by the Spirit to recognize Christian living not in terms of personal achievement but rather in showing others by our conduct what we already are because of God's gracious act of making us His saints.

The Call for Response

This particular passage begins with the word *therefore*. What does such a connection imply? It looks backward, does it not? In the present case, it connects what is now coming up for consideration with what has already been said about the actions God undertook for our salvation. These saving activities of the triune God have been the main theme of everything the apostle has written so far. God seeks us out with His offer of grace. To that grace of His we are then asked to respond in terms set forth in the passage before us. It is in this way that we show ourselves to be "obedient children" **(v. 14)**.

Readiness, steadiness, and a single-minded hope is what **verse 13** calls for. For the first of these items the apostle reaches back into the Old Testament for the way he puts his request. You will recall how the Israelites were directed by Moses **(Exodus 12:11)** to have their cloaks tucked in, their sandals on, and their staffs in hand on the night of the Passover. They were to be ready to move at a moment's notice. It is the kind of language Jesus Himself employed to exhort His followers to be ready at all times for His return. (Here see **Luke 12:35,** in particular).

The Lord's coming back is referred to also in **verse 13.** It is described in terms of grace heading our way to reach us at the moment when Jesus Christ will be revealed in His splendor. The prospect of such a stupendous happening might frighten anyone who thinks of it seriously. Hence the apostle also calls for both steadiness and a hope that is fully fixed on the liberation of God's children at the end of time.

There is another side to a proper response. It consists of not conforming to the lusts that characterize a pagan way of life and have their source in being ignorant of God's ways or deliberately ignoring them. The apostle, in his day, was writing to persons who, for the most part, had been won over to Christianity from total paganism, with all of its immorality and crude idolatry. Yet his exhortation of many centuries ago is as appropriate today as ever. For much of life in our society is not unlike the paganism of Peter's day. Sheer lust, religious ignorance, and outright idolatry prevail in large areas of life. As children of obedience—reborn to serve God—we are here asked to be different.

We are requested to shape our total conduct **(v. 15)** in keeping with the holiness of God who called us to be His children. It is by the Gospel that God calls us. That "good news is the account of what God has done for, in, and with us. Against this kind of background Peter sets forth the core principle of Christian ethics, namely, to shape our life in such a way as to be a response to God's actions. This is a way of saying that we should show ourselves to be what we already are: God's saints!

Father and Judge

It was customary in the early church to ask catechumens not to join in the Lord's Prayer until they had been fully instructed and baptized. In fact, they were usually dismissed from the worship service before Communion and the Lord's Prayer were offered. For, after all, the Lord's Prayer is the family prayer of the household of God; and it is by the Sacrament of Baptism that persons become members of that household.

Knowing God as Father—a new relationship established by God's call and the Baptism of the individual—a person might, in childlike confidence, forget the other side of God's holiness, namely, that He judges impartially. God cannot be bribed; He will not be impressed by rank, influence, status, or accomplishment.

His judgment is determined by what each one does with His faith. The apostle is very clear on this point when, in **verse 17,** he indicates that God judges each one impartially according to his or her performance. Peter is speaking of what Paul called "observing the law" **(Galatians 2:16),** by which people hope to gain God's favor by impressing Him with their piety. In **Peter,** as in the writings of Paul (see **Romans 2:6–7**), the reference is to what we do after we have come to faith and put it to work. What is our guide for knowing that what we do is good? It is the very same Law of God to which Jesus Himself was subject. (See **Galatians 4:4.**)

Set Free from Our Own Egypts

Peter sees a parallel in depth between the Israelites being set free and our being ransomed from the kind of Egypts people normally live in. He has already spoken of the ignorance of God and the evil desires that characterize life in general, before and without the new birth offered in Baptism (see **v. 14**). Now the apostle adds another item: sheer meaninglessness!

The phrase he uses is "empty way of life handed down to you from your forefathers" **(v. 18).** The converts to whom he was writing had grown up in a culture with a long history. Its values and goals had been handed down from generation to generation. Yet a close look at this past in light of the insight offered by God's Spirit revealed these ways as being empty of any abiding significance. All the past could be summed up in the words of the Preacher **(Ecclesiastes 1:2),** "Meaningless! Meaningless! . . . Everything is meaningless."

Life without a knowledge of the true God and a relationship of grace with Him is really quite pointless. It has as much meaning as Israelites making bricks for Pharaoh's taskmasters. God's ancient people were set free by God's power at the time of the first Passover. Peter now turns to this decisive event to describe the liberation that takes place by way of Baptism.

Christ, the True Passover Lamb

How does the word *precious*, as applied to the blood of our Lord **(v. 19),** keep us from thinking of God's grace as being cheap just because it is free to us?

Read **Exodus 12:3–6.** Note how the Passover lamb was set aside at one time of the month and slaughtered later. How does **verse 5** make the application to Jesus Christ?

The benefits of God's action in Christ are available to all. Yet they are appropriated only by those who come to faith **(v. 21).**

Such faith has as its object the God who raised Jesus from the dead and invested Him with glory. Anyone who accepts the fact of Jesus' resurrection and His ascension to the right hand of the Father will also realize that these events occurred to sound the Father's mighty "Amen!" over the suffering and death of our Lord as God's true Passover lamb.

Once again the apostle returns to the note of hope. And well he might! For the resurrection of Jesus Christ turns faith toward the future in hope.

For Group Discussion

1. Indicate in what way the fruit of the Spirit, as described in **Galatians 5:22–23,** cuts across our ordinary systems of values.

2. Comment on the application of **Hebrews 10:31** to **1 Peter 1:17.**

3. Give some reasons why great human virtues are not set forth in Scripture in terms of ideals to be achieved by us.

4. The story is told of how Benjamin Franklin kept a little notebook (diary) where he kept track of how he was doing each day in practicing certain virtues and avoiding certain vices. Is this an acceptable device for improvement in living a godly life?

A Glimpse Ahead

Next session we shall discuss life within the church as members of God's family.

Lesson 6

The Church as God's Family (1 Peter 1:22-25)

Our Goal Today

Our goal in this lesson is that we may be enlightened by the Spirit to grasp more fully the consequences of God's actions toward us as seen in terms of the relationship we have with our fellow redeemed.

Obedience to Truth

To be baptized is to respond in obedience to God's truth. Baptism comes up once more in **verse 22** by way of the expression, "you have purified yourselves." How did God command people to use water in **Exodus 19:10** or **Leviticus 17:15?**

Verse 22 is not speaking of any outward washing; rather it is the souls of the readers that have been purified. That the reference is to Baptism becomes obvious from the next verse **(23),** where the apostle speaks of having been born again. How do you understand this washing of the soul? **(v. 22)?**

Truth is one of the mighty words of Scripture. It does not occur in the plural since the truth of God is one. It is a word to describe God as relating Himself to us as one who is utterly reliable. There is no shadow of deceit in any promise He has ever made or any other word He has spoken through His prophets, apostles, and evangelists. Jesus described Himself as "the way and the truth and the life **(John 14:6).**

Truth consists of more than raw facts. It reaches out from one person to another in the expectation of being believed. *Obedience* is one word for such a response. It means "listening and accepting." Peter describes his readers as having done just that. They had purified their souls by such obedience to what God had spoken and promised.

To Be God's Family

Baptism does not take place in a vacuum. Souls are purified for a "sincere love for your brothers." By Baptism persons become sons and daughters of God and as such are brothers and sisters in God's family, where love is to be manifested by one to the other.

As the apostle wrote the word *love*, he did not have in mind the sentimental kind of emotion often associated with that word in our language. He used the Greek word *agape* (ah-GAH-pay) to make his point; and that is basically an action of the will! The agape kind of love is determined never to break off communication and offers itself to the other person with a view to service. It is used of God loving us first.

Such love reaches out to what is not worth loving. (See how Paul makes this point in **Romans 5:10.**) Such love, moreover, is always prepared to be betrayed. God's Son knew beforehand that He would be rejected by the majority of His very own. Yet He became incarnate. The prospect of being put to death did not deter Him in the task of redeeming us.

Showing that kind of love toward others of the household of faith is at times hard work. Hence the apostle adds the word *deeply* (*earnestly* [RSV]). Earnestly is a term used to describe Jesus praying in the garden **(Luke 22:44).** Such love just never lets go and is to be practiced without hypocrisy.

Born Again

Just as we had no voice in our first birth, so any contribution on our part to being born all over again is excluded. Peter, as well as Jesus Himself (see **John 3:4–8**), emphasizes that our rebirth is completely God's work in us.

Like the Returning Remnant

Peter's quote of **Isaiah 40:6–8** is very apt.

Babylon, to which the tribes of Benjamin and Judah were taken into captivity, radiated the splendor of any civilized city and great culture. The Roman Empire was known for its similar splendor.

All such glory, however, is like "the flowers of the field," which wither and fall. For, in the last analysis, all flesh—everything that people are and do—is like grass. The prophet reminded God's ancient exiles of this elementary fact, inviting them to return to the hard frontier of their homeland with a view to resettling Jerusalem and rebuilding the temple on Mount Zion. The word he had from the God of Israel, he insisted, would outlast all of Babylon's splendor. In fact, it would abide forever, since the Light of the nations, the Savior of humankind, would come from Bethlehem and Jerusalem and not from Babylon.

Comparatively speaking, only a few took the prophet at his word. Just a remnant returned; the rest preferred the comforts and conveniences offered by the land to which they had been exiled. Who, in his right mind, would have thought that the future of humanity lay with a handful of people slowly wending their way back to the rugged stone and hostile hillsides of Palestine? Yet that is the way God works. His grace chooses the weak and lowly to accomplish His purposes.

The Christians to whom Peter sent his letter found themselves in a situation much like that of the Jews in exile. Power and splendor were all on the side of Rome, which later on **(1 Peter 5:13)** is called Babylon. Why should they cut themselves off from its system of values and its way of life? Was it really worthwhile?

It is precisely such questions that the apostle chose to answer by reaching back into the Old Testament for a word to a faithful remnant of many centuries before.

For Group Discussion

1. Does Christian love extend to people outside the household of God? In what way?

2. What is the role of the Apostles' Creed in Holy Baptism?

3. Why is it necessary to know and use such statements as included in the Nicene and Athanasian Creeds?

4. In what way is contemporary secularism a greater hazard to faith than the harassment and persecutions suffered by the persons to whom Peter first wrote this letter?

A Glimpse Ahead

We must always carefully distinguish between God's goodness and His grace. The next lesson will consider the difference between the two.

Lesson 7

The Place of God's Presence in Grace
(1 Peter 2:1–8)

Our Goal Today

Our goal in this lesson is that we may grow in our appreciation and gratitude for the arrangements God Himself made to be present among us in His grace.

Presence in Grace

The original Greek word for "rid yourselves" means "to shed one's clothes" as those early Christians did when they were baptized by immersion. (Check **Romans 13:12–14; James 1:21; Colossians 3:8; Ephesians 4:22–25;** and **Hebrews 12:1.**) In Baptism, people replace the "clothing" of their former way of life with the "cloak" of Christ's righteousness.

Baptism is one means of grace. What are the other two?

Where are they mentioned in **verses 1–3?**

A New Kind of Community

Sociologists are fond of the term *community*. But we are here dealing with an apostolic document and not with a brief on social structures. Here the word occurs in our heading to alert us to the various ways in which Peter describes Christians as related to each other. If you will quickly scan verses **4–8,** you will meet at least two: *house* and *priesthood*. Priests bring people near to God by interceding for them. At what point does a congregation do this in its public (Sunday) services?

House, in this context, is another word for temple. The sanctuary on Mount Zion, which Peter knew from the earlier years in his life, was built of magnificent stone and shining gold. It was a material house. The church, each congregation, is a spiritual edifice, made up of people in whom and among whom God's Spirit lives and works. Instead of the cloud of glory that used to hover above the ark of the covenant in the days of the Jerusalem temple **(Leviticus 16:2),** we have God's own Spirit present with us.

Moved by that Spirit the church offers up such "spiritual sacrifices" as prayer, praise, thanksgiving, works of love, and offerings of material things. The best of them all is that of individuals offering themselves to God totally as "living sacrifices" **(Romans 12:1).**

The Cornerstone

That spiritual house in which each Christian is a building stone, so to speak, is constructed around Jesus Christ as the cornerstone **(vv. 5–6).** What purpose does a cornerstone serve in a modern-day building?

The Stone of Stumbling

In the days of Jesus and His apostles the Jews told the story of a massive stone over which people of old kept stumbling as they were trying to build Solomon's temple. It was very much in the way until some prophet came along to point out to the builders that this particular stone would serve as a solid cornerstone. It was then quickly put into place. It fit; and the erection of that ancient sanctuary could proceed.

Whether or not Peter had this story in mind is impossible to demonstrate. Nor does it matter whether he did or not. This thought of builders stumbling over a stone that became the capstone was expressed in **Psalm 118:22;** and this had been sung at every Passover Peter had attended in his lifetime. Look up **Matthew 16:23** to see how Jesus used these very words about Himself. Who were "the builders" in Jesus' day?

Who are the builders in our day?

What They Were Destined For

The last clause of **verse 8** has at times been used to argue for double predestination, meaning that, as God has chosen some for eternal life, He destined others to destruction. How do you react to such an interpretation? (See **1 Timothy 2:4** to help you.)

What the apostle actually meant to convey was the connection between unbelief and stumbling. Where there is an unwillingness to take God at His Word, people keep stumbling over the one chosen by Him to be the very head of the corner. God is not the problem; people are, when they reject His offer of grace. "They stumble," wrote the apostle, "because they disobey the message" **(v. 8).** It is as simple and as frightening as that.

For Group Discussion

1. Show the difference between Paul's use **(Romans 9:33)** of the Old Testament quotation about the stone and Peter's way of handling it in the passage under study.

2. In what sense would Jesus Christ be called the "living Stone" in **verse 5?** Relate this to the concept of "living hope" in **1:3.**

3. Is the mode of Baptism (immersion, sprinkling, pouring) of importance? What are the dynamic factors at work in this Sacrament?

A Glimpse Ahead

In the next lesson we will consider the major task for which the church has been created.

Lesson 8

A People Belonging to God
(1 Peter 2:9–12)

Our Goal Today

Our goal in this lesson is that we may become more sensitive to the purposes for which God went to so much bother in order to make us His own.

Corporate Calling

The apostle, in **verse 9,** once more reaches back into the Old Testament: **Exodus 19:5–6.** Note the difference in wording but similarity in substance between the **Exodus** passage and **verse 9** here. God spoke the words in **Exodus,** through Moses, to Israel at Mount Sinai. By way of the waters of the Red Sea this people had been baptized "into Moses," as Paul tells us in **1 Corinthians 10:2.** In this way they became children of God's grace.

Among this people God arranged to set up the tabernacle, where sacrifices were offered in expectation of that one great shedding of blood, which took place on Calvary. In other words, God offered forgiveness at the tent of meeting by way of the rites and sacrifices established there. That is where priests prayed; where they drew near to God and brought God to His people. For God had chosen this people and made them His: "a people belonging to God" **(verse 9).** The Hebrew word used in **Exodus 19:5–6** connotes something precious, like the chosen cornerstone referred to in the previous lesson.

As a nation Israel was called to be "holy." This does not mean that it was offered a set of high ethical ideals to achieve or else perish. At the heart of *holiness* is the thought of separation for service. Israel was chosen from among the nations of the world for exclusive service to the true God. (Here review for yourself the First Commandment and be ready to recite it. How does this commandment define holiness?)

The corporate aspect of God's people, the church, is depicted once more in **verse 10a.** Here the allusion is to Hosea, whose book is, without a doubt, the most eloquent commentary on God's faithfulness in the face of His own people's disobedience.

Hosea's adulterous wife **(Hosea 1:2)** bore him three children: a son named Jezreel, which means "God scatters"; a daughter who was named "Not Loved"; and a son named Lo-Ammi ("Not My People"). These three children symbolized the fallen estate of Israel, which had forgotten and even rejected God's covenant. And yet God, in His steadfast love, regathered His people, turned "Not My People" into His people and "Not Loved" into a daughter to whom He extended mercy.

Peter turns this prophetic vocabulary and symbolism to his own apostolic use, indicating that his readers were once not a people at all. They had nothing really worthwhile in common. Each went his or her own way after the fashion of wandering sheep (as he puts it in **verse 25** in this chapter). But now, as newly baptized children of God, they had all experienced God's mercy and become His own people.

Continuity in Action

It is helpful, in this context, to analyze the model of the action God took at Sinai to establish Israel as a holy nation. It has six facets, which repeat themselves in the ministry of Jesus and the creation of the church.

In the **first** instance, Israel was created as an act of **God's grace.** This people did not deserve to be chosen as God's precious possession. **Deuteronomy 7:6–8** tells us that in so many words.

We have already noted that God selected a whole nation, a racial **community** to be His kingdom of priests. That is the **second** element in this model.

Third, Israel became the **place of God's presence** in grace. All of the second half of **Exodus** is devoted to a description of this tent of meeting, where God chose to meet with and speak to His people, particularly at the ark of the covenant, the altar of burnt offering, and the altar of incense.

Fourth, the Israelites were expected to **obey** God's will **(Exodus 19:5).**

Living in such a close relationship with God, Israel was given the mission to bring this knowledge of God to other nations. Where such contact with the people of the living God was opposed, judgment followed. Only such individuals as Rahab (**Joshua 6:17**) and her family were saved from the destruction that engulfed Jericho even as it had the Moabites and Amorites before that. God is a holy Lord and will, therefore, not tolerate rejection of His offer of grace. **Israel's mission** and **God's judgment** constitute the **fifth** and **sixth** sides of this hexagonal (six-cornered) model.

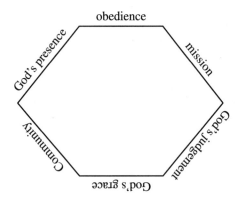

Now apply this model to the life and works of Jesus, point by point, and to the church, the new Israel.

Declare the Praises

How does **verse 9b** apply to what happens in Baptism?

Noble Conduct

As "aliens and strangers" **(vv. 11–12)** we Christians are in the world but not of it. Hence our conduct will be different from that of unbelievers (pagans). A shining lifestyle will tend to contradict the bad things often said about and to God's children. It may even bring some to the point of joining in glorifying God for the "good deeds" they observe on the part of Christians.

Share with the class some examples of heartwarming deeds done by Christians you know. (Perhaps members of your own family? neighborhood? church?)

For Group Discussion

1. How do you relate God's judgment to His grace?

2. Describe specifically how the conduct of Christians differs noticeably from the unbelieving world around us.

3. What does it mean to "glorify God"?

4. Name the "sinful desires" from which God's children are directed to abstain.

A Glimpse Ahead

How God's people relate to such institutions of society as government, the economic order, and matrimony: these matters will be considered in the next lesson.

Lesson 9

Attitude toward Government and Economic Systems (1 Peter 2:13–25)

Our Goal Today

Our goal in this lesson is that we may be moved to relate ourselves properly to the institutions of government and of economic systems as orders of preservation.

In the World but Not of It

In **2:13–3:12** Peter speaks of the "orders of creation" (or preservation). This is a phrase used of those institutions in society that make it possible for life to go on in a reasonably ordered way. The three important ones are government, the economic order, and matrimony.

The Key Term: Submit

What comes to your mind when you hear the word *submit?*

What is really meant by "submit yourselves" **(v. 13)** is an act of faith whereby Christians rank themselves and their own needs under those of others. As St. Paul put it: "Each of you should look not only to your own interests, but also to the interests of others" **(Philippians 2:4).**

Peter speaks of "authority instituted among men." God created these human institutions for the benefit of a fallen world, where nothing but the law of the jungle would prevail were it not for the institutions of government, economic arrangements, and matrimony.

There need not be anything demeaning about submitting, for our Lord Himself did so (see **Luke 2:51; 1 Corinthians 15:28; Philippians 2:7).** And we are to submit ourselves "for the Lord's sake."

Toward Government

In Rome itself he was called Caesar; but out in the provinces, to which Peter sent this epistle, the chief ruler was known as king or emperor. He represented and controlled the government of that time. He had the authority to send out governors to "punish those who do wrong and to commend those who do right." They administered parts of the empire for Caesar.

We have no emperors ruling us. We elect our officials. But that does not change our responsibility of being submissive to them; for whatever authorities exist have been instituted by God **(Romans 13:1).** This being the case, Christians are called upon to do God's will "by doing good" **(v. 15).** Peter has in mind the practice of loyalty toward government: paying taxes, helping in public projects, strengthening the structures of justice, and the like.

To what extent do we have even greater opportunities for "doing good" than the early Christians did under Caesar's police state?

Christians were (and are) often accused of disloyalty for appealing to an authority higher than that of government in cases where they are ordered to do something contrary to God's Law. But they can "silence the ignorant talk of foolish men" by their outstanding citizenship. In this way they demonstrate that they are servants of God, who understand the strange paradox of their own freedom, namely, that such freedom consists in service, such as honoring all people, loving the believers, fearing God, and honoring the king **(v. 17).** God would have us serve as good citizens, promoting and exercising the very freedom to which He has called us.

Toward Economic Systems

No society could exist for more than a few months without some kind of economic structures. Hence any such arrangements belong to the order of preservation, making life in community possible even though this is a world where most people are out to get all they can for themselves.

The Roman Empire depended on slave labor just as we depend on machines to do most of our hard work. To that situation the apostle addressed himself. He did not advocate revolution but submission even to surly and overbearing masters **(v. 18).**

In that context Peter gives expression to a radically new and Christian principle. Read **verse 20.** The noblest example of this is none other than Jesus Christ Himself, hence the apostle calls for imitating Jesus **(v. 21).** Can you think of specific examples?

Have you had any experiences of this kind? Explain.

For Healing

Peter has the exciting habit of inserting into ethical contexts statements of pure doctrine dealing with the very heart of our faith. He does so here, in **verses 24–25,** to point up the connection between belief and practice.

Explain how there can be healing in the practice of what the apostle calls submission!

For Group Discussion

1. At the time of the U.S. War of Independence many Lutherans and Episcopalians moved to Canada rather than take part in the revolution. Were they right?

2. In our interpretation of this section we have distinguished between what is contingent (like emperors and slaves) and what is constant (the institutions of government and economic systems). Can you think of other instances where such a distinction becomes crucial for a proper understanding of Scripture?

3. Do Christians who belong to labor unions have a right to strike? How does the distinction between the kingdom of God's left hand and of His right hand become decisive in answering that question?

A Glimpse Ahead

In the next session we consider the order of preservation called matrimony.

Lesson 10

Life in the Married Estate and in the Church (1 Peter 3:1-12)

Our Goal Today

Our goal in this lesson that we may be guided, on the basis of God's Word, to develop a more profound sense of sacrifice and service within the context of matrimony as an order of preservation and of the church (congregation) as belonging to the order of redemption.

Husbands and Wives

Peter was a married man (see **1 Corinthians 9:5**). No doubt his wife was a follower of the Lord, perhaps since even before Jesus miraculously healed her mother **(Mark 1:30–31).** By inspiration of the Spirit Peter wrote, therefore, as one who knew both the joys and the problems of the married estate.

The lot of Christian wives was most difficult in the ancient world, especially when they became members of the church and their husbands did not. Hence six of the seven verses that deal with marriage are devoted to the responsibilities and attitudes of wives.

How do **verses 1 and 2** imply that Peter had in mind Christian wives with pagan husbands?

"Purity and reverence" **(v. 2)** are not means of grace. Ordinarily the knowledge of salvation comes only as we speak the Gospel. Yet a Christian's conduct may make the other person more willing to listen. Marriage, of course, is such an intimate estate that at times nothing at all needs to be said in order to convey a message. At times, in fact, not saying anything may express most eloquently what needs to be communicated! At any rate, incessant chatter can be self-defeating. Faith and salvation are too important to be forfeited that way.

Inner Attitude

How could **verse 3** be completely misunderstood if it were read without its context?

The apostle was interested in matters that do not perish because they are precious in God's sight. Fancy hairdos, expensive jewelry, and flashy clothes do not belong to that category. They are very perishable; indeed, God cannot be impressed by outward appearances, for He is a God that sees right through to what is inside the heart.

Fellow Heirs

In **verse 7** the apostle turns to the subject of husbands. Since he was writing to newly baptized Christians, his words are intended for husbands who have been born again by water and the Spirit. He appeals to them to "be considerate" with their wives. Here the King James Version is more correct in translating "according to knowledge."

The knowledge is that of God and His ways of salvation. At the same time it includes an understanding of the way God created Eve as a helper for Adam. Knowing this, a Christian husband learns to put a new value on his wife, and this, in turn, finds expression in the honor a husband accords his wife as a fellow heir of eternal life.

Suppose we lived in a society where women (wives) had no right to inherit anything. Then a message would be proclaimed making them fellow heirs of eternal life. How radical do you think that would sound?

Imagine what it meant to say in that kind of setting that men were to live with their wives as fellow heirs of eternal life! Such language is like the yeast implanted in "a large amount of flour" (see **Matthew 13:33**) that changed the lot of women to a degree that neither Plato nor Seneca would have dreamed of—or even encouraged!

Harmony

What do **verses 8–9** tell us about life in the church? Use your own words for an interpretation.

For Group Discussion

1. Should the word *obey* be retained in the marriage vows spoken by the bride? Why or why not?

2. What is meant by the statement that in marriage a man and a woman become one flesh **(Ephesians 5:31)?**

3. In what ways is the sacredness of the married estate being threatened today?

4. Among the ancient Greeks and Romans humility was considered to be the attitude of slaves and therefore unworthy of a free citizen. Comment on humility as God empowers us to demonstrate it.

A Glimpse Ahead

In the next lesson we will look at life under the lordship of Jesus Christ.

Lesson 11

Life under the Lordship of Jesus Christ (1 Peter 3:13–22)

Our Goal Today

Our goal in this lesson is that we may be led to realize more fully how discipleship often brings with it a large measure of suffering, and that this is part of following one who Himself suffered and died but then rose again, thereby establishing His lordship not only over heavenly powers but also over the nether regions.

Doing Good May Bring on Suffering

Verse 13 reads like the kind of question that answers itself. The response ought to be a simple, "No one!" But Christian life does not come that simply. Doing what is good and right in the eyes of God (righteous living) at times brings on suffering in terms of harassment and even persecution.

Under such difficult conditions, Peter asks the Lord's disciples at all times to be prepared to give an answer when asked why they believe and act the way they do (**vv. 14–15**). The apostle calls this "the hope that you have." We might have expected the word *faith*, but Peter prefers the term *hope*, which really means "faith turned toward the future."

It is difficult, even impossible, to give an account of one's convictions unless they have been learned well and thought through very carefully. That is one of the major reasons for having confirmation instruction and engaging in Bible study. How would you fare, for example, right now if some enemies of the Christian religion were to put you to the test? Would you be able to explain the hope that is in you the way the church's martyrs did and do? If not, why not?

With Gentleness and Respect

A gentle and respectful response to persecution can produce, as **verse 16** points out, shame and frustration of the kind experienced by Annas, Caiaphas, Pilate, and Herod when Jesus was brought to trial before them. As long as anyone was still willing to listen, our Lord was ready to respond; He fell into silence when it became obvious that further talking was pointless. Before Herod He declined to say anything. Even His silence put to shame those who were mocking Him. Jesus' example illustrates the truth of **verse 17.**

In what way did Stephen imitate his Lord? (Skim **Acts 6:11–7:60.**)

Our Model and Warrantor

What does **verse 18** tell us about Jesus' death? Mention at least two results that are indicated in this verse.

"Bring you to God" is an expression that suggests the act of a royal person admitting someone into his or her presence. It took nothing less than the death of God's Son to remove the obstacle of sin that separates us from God!

Note the word *Spirit* in **verse 18.** Although this may be referring to the Holy Spirit, it is more likely meant to be Christ's own spirit. Jesus Christ was brought back to life with respect to His spirit in the same sense as Jairus' daughter's spirit returned to her when Jesus brought her back to life **(Luke 8:55).**

What do you make of **verse 19?** Explain it in your own words.

Christ has overcome death, the devil, and eternal damnation. We have this confidence as a major ingredient of our life under the lordship of Jesus Christ. Having triumphed over death and hell, Christ is the warrantor of eternal life with Him.

Flood-Baptism

The flood of Noah's day **(v. 20)** is a prototype of how Baptism works: it saves by water. **Verse 21** is translated "the pledge [or response] of a good conscience toward God." This translation does not do full justice to the expression used by the original text. Peter used a term that referred to the questions asked as a contract was being drawn up and agreed upon. The word suggests the kind of questions put to individuals during the rite of Baptism. What are some of those questions your sponsors or you were asked?

Both questions and responses are involved. That is the way Baptism works, says the apostle. In that way Baptism saves people by one resurrection of Jesus Christ; for being baptized means appropriating all the benefits available through the risen Lord.

How does **Revelation 19:16** apply to **verse 22?**

In Baptism we have the name of our God the Father, Son, and Holy Spirit written on us. It is this very name that gives us access to life under the mighty lordship of Jesus Christ!

For Group Discussion

1. Cite individual instances of suffering for being a Christian.

2. "God's right hand is everywhere" (Formula of Concord, Epitome, VII, 12). How does this statement prove helpful for our understanding of the Lord's Supper?

A Glimpse Ahead

In the next lesson we will look at how we, as members of God's redeemed people, belong to a suffering and serving community.

Lesson 12

A Suffering and a Serving Community (1 Peter 4:1-19)

Our Goal Today

Our goal in this lesson is that we may be enlightened by the Spirit to comprehend, with growing appreciation, how we, as members of God's redeemed people, may be exposed to the ridicule and harassment of the world, and how, precisely under such circumstances, we are to serve in imitation of Jesus Christ.

Baptism: End of Chapter One

In this whole epistle the word *Baptism* occurs only once. Do you recall how it was used in **3:21?** Now read **4:1-6.**

Even though the term itself is given in just one passage, most of Peter's letter deals with this Sacrament: its power, its effectiveness, and its results. The first six verses of **chapter 4** flow from the apostle's previous mention of Baptism. They show that persons who have been baptized into Christ, including His suffering, now live in a new era of their own personal lives. Former ways of doing things have been done away with. The change is so radical that it surprises the people who had known the believers before as persons ready to join them in all the immoral and godless practices that characterize worldly living **(v. 4).** Peter was writing to congregations whose members had been won over from a totally pagan way of life, where gross idolatry, drinking bouts, bawdy religious processions, and the crass pursuit of lust and pleasure were openly accepted and practiced.

In the case of his original audience, Peter points out that the Good News was proclaimed to the first-generation Christians in order that they might know of the glory awaiting them beyond whatever judgment other people might reach in their cases. This seems to be the best way to understand **verse 6.** The dead in this verse are Christians who seemed dead as a result of human judgment over them. It was due to the work of the Gospel that, despite harassment and persecution, they could and would live "according to God in regard to the spirit." These words suggest that new dimension of everlasting life in the Spirit, which has already begun for those who believe and are baptized. (See **Mark 16:16.**)

Pressures of the End Time

Read the second section of this chapter: **verses 7–11.**

The thought of all things coming to an end might frighten some and mislead others. Peter, therefore, asks his readers to keep clear minded and self-controlled in order to carry on a proper prayer life. Then he returns to the practice of love as the item of highest priority: love for one another.

Why does love rate so high? Because it has a way of covering up any number of sins and faults we may see in the other person. It takes a great deal of determination to practice such selfless love. That is why the apostle urges believers to love "deeply" **(v. 8).** The term literally means "fervently." Loving other people, even other Christians, takes effort and requires a great deal of determination, including the ungrumbling practice of hospitality **(v. 9).**

Verses 10–11 set forth a fundamental operating principle for any and every Christian congregation, namely, that the various gifts with which the Holy Spirit endows individuals are to be used for one another in terms of mutual edification. This is a matter of being good stewards of "God's grace in its various forms."

Peter then mentions two such general gifts of grace. Which are they? In what sequence are they mentioned **(v. 11)?**

Do you think there is any significance in the order? (Compare the sequence in **Mark 2:1–12.**)

As the apostle reflects on the possibilities and potentials of this new way of life, he breaks out in the words of a doxology.

Suffering with Christ

What picture comes to your mind at the mention of a "painful trial" (**v. 12**)?

Which thoughts in **verses 12–19** seem most significant to you?

For Group Discussion

1. Apply the first six verses of **chapter 4** to those baptized as infants.

2. What gifts of the Spirit can you see at work in your congregation in terms of service to one another?

3. Comment on the statement written by George MacDonald, the teacher of C. S. Lewis: "The Son of Man suffered death, not that men might not suffer, but that their suffering might be like His."

4. In what way do you think Christians who suffer for their faith find comfort in **1 Peter 4:17–19?**

A Glimpse Ahead

In the final chapter of this book the apostle takes up the theme of the church as God's flock.

Lesson 13

We Are God's Flock
(1 Peter 5:1–14)

Our Goal Today

Our goal in this lesson is that we may be moved to practice such virtues as are appropriate to our status as members of God's flock.

Shepherding God's Flock

The "elders" (v. 1) were the pastors of the various churches to which Peter was writing. Note that Peter did not hesitate to consider himself to be a fellow elder, all of them under the tutelage and rule of the Chief Shepherd of them all, Jesus Christ (v. 4).

Having been at the Transfiguration (Mark 9:2–8), Peter had had a glimpse of the glory that will in time be revealed as the privilege and destiny of all those who follow the Chief Shepherd! The apostle was also a witness to Christ's suffering, some of which he personally saw, most of which he missed either by falling asleep or by running away from the scene of his Lord's agony and abuse.

These first verses of **chapter five** remind all those in charge of a Christian congregation that it is God's flock, not their own, they are tending. The wrong way to go about the responsibilities that go with such a calling is to want to use the office for gain or for power. Since it is a task of rare privilege, no one ought to assume it under constraint but rather with the same kind of eagerness with which God undertook our salvation in the first place. What is involved in the task of shepherding?

Pastors are expected to be models for their flocks. How can they best do so?

The Art of Humility

The exhortation of **verse 5** describes the way the Lord Himself dealt with His disciples. He clothed Himself with a towel to wash their feet **(John 13:4)** as a way of underlining the servanthood to which He was calling them in imitation of His own example. (Tell as much as you can about that first Maundy Thursday!)

Ancient pagan philosophers despised humility as being the virtue only slaves would practice. But they did not know our Lord who humbled Himself so that His Father might exalt Him in due time **(Philippians 2:5–9)**. To the practice of this very kind of humbleness in spirit the apostle directs us **(v. 6)**, reminding us that the power and the right to raise a person up to heights of exaltation lie in the hand of God. God's hand or His arm are standard symbols in Scripture for the Lord Himself reaching into life and history to do the unexpected, such as calling an ancient slave people to be His very own. Since He is that kind of God, He is fully capable of taking whatever anxieties and burdens we may carry and carry them Himself. In fact, He is happy to do so since, as the apostle says very explicitly, "He cares for you" **(v. 7)**.

Danger All Around

To want to destroy anything and everything that God creates lies at the very center of all that our "enemy" **(v. 8)** plans and carries out. Can you recall an incident in which Peter fell prey to the Evil One?

Christians are to be self-controlled and alert. They are called on to resist Satan's every approach. He has a way of discovering the weak points in any life and does not hesitate to take advantage of them, especially by means of sinful desires, which were described in **2:11** as waging open warfare against the soul. Christian living, therefore, is a call to watchfulness, resistance, and steadfastness in the faith.

With such dangers all around, it is no small source of comfort to have at one's beck and call a Savior who is eager to reach in with His strong right hand to keep us from becoming victims of Satan's wiles. Having such divine assistance available offers no guarantee that any follower of Jesus Christ will escape suffering. Once more the apostle returns to this theme, reminding his readers that "the same kind of sufferings" (**v. 9**) are required of the total family of God, wherever its members are and in whatever age they may be living.

Glory!

However, the Good Friday of suffering is the prelude to an Easter of glory. In fact, without Good Friday there would be no Easter. Accordingly, while God does, indeed, permit His children to suffer, it lasts only "a little while" (**v. 10**). What follows is everlasting. And we are expressly told that it is God's intent to restore, to establish, and to strengthen His children so that they may attain to that glory for which they were called in Christ.

Throughout this epistle Peter has spoken of the glory that follows suffering. The example he offers is that of Jesus Christ: His suffering and glorification. Is it worthwhile, therefore, to belong to God's assembly of saints? We will recall that this is the practical question to which this whole epistle is directed. By the time we reach the end, it is possible to answer that haunting query with a loud yes! Therefore, says the apostle, to God be the power for ever and ever (**v. 11**)!

Conclusion

Note (**v. 12**) how highly Peter commends Silas, also known as Silvanus, whom he had himself, without a doubt, chosen to do the tedious work of printing out on papyrus or leather, word for word, what the apostle was inspired to write to the congregations in the provinces mentioned in the salutation. Furthermore, Silas was also Peter's personal representative in bringing and reading this epistle to the various congregations involved.

"My son Mark" **(v. 13)** no doubt refers to John Mark, the apostle's spiritual son and disciple. While this Mark was often in the company of Paul (see **Colossians 4:10**), he is also known from ancient sources as Peter's follower and interpreter. He wrote the gospel that still bears his name.

The "kiss of love" **(v. 14)** is still part of the communion liturgy in the Eastern church. Phillips translates, "Give each other a handshake all round as a sign of love," which is the more common custom in congregations in western countries.

Justified through faith **(Romans 5:1)**, we have the "peace" that Peter speaks of in **verse 14.**

For Group Discussion

1. Why do we not carry out literally the directive to "greet one another with a kiss of love"? How does our failure to carry out this directive literally compare to our not washing each other's feet, for which Jesus set us an example?

2. The devil is here called our "enemy." What else do the Scriptures call him?

3. For what twofold purpose did Peter write this letter? Read **verses 12–14.**

1 PETER
God's Chosen People

Leaders Notes

Leaders Notes

Preparing to Teach 1 Peter

Group Bible Study

Group Bible study means mutual learning from one another under the guidance of a leader or facilitator. The Bible is an inexhaustible resource. No one person can discover all it has to offer. In a class, many eyes see many things, and can apply them to many life situations. Leaders should resist the temptation to "give the answers" and thereby take on the role of an "authority." This approach stifles participation by individual members and can actually hamper learning. As a general rule, the leader is not to give interpretation, but to *develop interpreters*. Of course, there are times when leaders should and must share insights and information gained by their own deeper research.

The ideal class is one in which the leader guides class members through the lesson, engages them in meaningful sharing and discussion at all points, and leads them to a summary of the lesson at the conclusion. As a general rule, try to avoid telling learners things that they can discover by themselves.

Have a chalkboard and chalk or newsprint and marker available to note significant points of the lesson. Recast your observations about the lesson, or the observations of participants, into questions, problems, or issues. This stimulates thought and reflection. Keep discussion to the point. List on the chalkboard or newsprint the answers given. Then determine the most vital points made in the discussion. Ask additional questions to fill obvious gaps.

The aim of every Bible study is to help people grow spiritually, not merely in biblical and theological knowledge, but in Christian thinking and living. This means growth in Christian attitudes, insights, and skills for Christian living. The focus of this course must be the church and world of our day. The guiding question will be, "What does the Lord teach us for life today through this letter of Peter?"

Teaching the New Testament

Teaching a New Testament letter that was originally written for and read to first-century Christians can become merely ancient history if not applied to life in our times. Leaders need to understand the time and culture in which the letter was written. They need to understand the historical situation of the early church and the social and cultural setting in which that church existed. Such background information can clarify the original purpose and meaning of the letters and shed light on their meaning for Christians today. For this reason, it would be good to consult a number of commentaries and Bible reference works in preparation for class.

Teaching the Bible can easily degenerate into mere moralizing, in which do-goodism or rules become substitutes for the Gospel, and sanctification is confused with justification. Actually, justified sinners are moved, not by Law, but by God's grace to a totally new life. Their faith is always at work for Christ in every context of life. Meaningful personal Christianity consists in a loving trust in God that is evidenced in love for others. Having experienced God's free grace and forgiveness, Christians daily work in their world to reflect the will of God for people in every area of human endeavor.

Christian leaders are Gospel-oriented, not Law-oriented: they distinguish between the two. Both Law and Gospel are necessary. The Gospel will mean nothing unless we first have been crushed by the Law and see our sinfulness. There is no genuine Christianity if faith is not followed by lives pleasing to God. In fact, genuine faith is inseparable from life. The Gospel alone gives us the new heart that causes us to love God and our neighbor.

Pace Your Teaching

Do not try to cover every question in each lesson. This would lead to undue haste and frustration. Be selective. Know your class members and pace your teaching accordingly. Take time to explore the biblical text, but do not focus on every minute detail. Rather, get the sweep and continuity of meaning. Stop occasionally to help participants gain understanding of a word or concept. Encourage members to study the text at home and report their findings at the next session. The time gained can be used to apply the lesson to life.

Should your group have more than a one-hour class period, you can ease the pace and proceed with more leisure. But do not allow any lesson to "drag" and become tiresome. Keep things moving. Keep the class alive. Keep the lesson meaningful.

Good Preparation

Good preparation by the leader usually affects the pleasure and satisfaction the class will experience. The student or teacher cannot get the background—historical, cultural, and theological—for **1 Peter** by reading only the biblical text. Paragraphs, sentences, phrases, individual words and expressions can be understood fully only in light of the times and circumstances in which the apostle wrote. Thus it is important that both student and class leader consult introductory articles in reference works and commentaries. Also read the text in another translation.

Parishes should provide leaders with some essential books by purchasing them for the church library or for the individual teacher's library. The following resources are especially recommended:

- a good, recently revised Bible dictionary or encyclopedia;
- a thorough Bible commentary such as *The People's Bible* from Concordia Publishing House;
- one or more recent translations and paraphrases of Peter's letter: NIV, NRSV, Phillips, *The Living Bible.*

Personal Preparation

Good teaching directs the learners to discover for themselves. For the leader, this means directing learners, not giving answers. As you prepare, mark those sections which suggest an activity most suitable for your class. Choose verses that should be looked up in Scripture. Decide which discussion questions you will ask, and to which you will devote the most time Write these in the margins of your Leader's Guide. Highlight the Study Guide questions you'll emphasize. What practical actions could you propose for the week following the lesson? Which group-discussion questions in the Study Guide do you feel are most appropriate for your class? Mark these in your book.

Plan brief opening and closing devotions. Either use the suggestions provided in the Leader's Guide, or make up your own devotions. As much as possible—especially after the first sessions, when participants may still feel uncomfortable—involve class members in these devotions.

How will you best use your teaching period? Do you have 45 minutes? An hour? Or 1 1/2 hours? If time is short, what should you cut? Learn to become a wise steward of class time.

Perhaps most important of all, be sure to begin your preparations for each session—and the class sessions themselves—with personal prayer. Ask for God's wisdom, direction, and insight so that your mind is freed to focus on the biblical material and what it says to your life. When the text becomes clear to you, when Peter's words have meaning for your *life*, you will find it exciting—exhilarating—to help your class members discover how this letter speaks to them.

Suggestions for Using the Study Guide

This set of 13 lessons is based on a significant and timely New Testament writing—Peter's letter to Christians who are experiencing the trials of persecution. The Study Guide material is designed to aid Bible study: that is, to aid a consideration of the written Word of God, with discussion and personal application growing out of the text at hand. Don't hesitate to alter the suggestions or to substitute other ideas that will better meet your own needs and the needs of the participants. Adapt your teaching plan to your own class and your class period.

Begin your first class session by reading to the class the Overall Aims of the Course, which follows. Then let the class briefly respond to two questions: "What do you expect to get out of this course in the light of these aims?" and "In what way does our being here in this group further the aim that is numbered as III B 4?"

Overall Aims of the Course

I. To provide the occasion for deepening our understanding and heightening our appreciation of the privileged status we enjoy as God's redeemed children by virtue of the following:
   A. God's gracious choice of us in eternity.
   B. His "mighty acts" within history to implement His selection of us
      1. in continuity with God's people of the Old Covenant; and
      2. in succession to God's ancient people of Israel.
II. To offer the opportunity to develop a sharpened awareness of the nature of our life in response to God's choice and actions in terms of its
   A. content;
   B. direction; and
   C. style.
III. To create a situation of individuals gathered as an assembly around God's Word and so to do the following:
   A. Exhibit the presence of God's people at a particular place engaged in
      1. searching the Scriptures;
      2. edifying each other; and
      3. maturing in their faith.
   B. Acknowledge the presence of God at work through His Spirit by
      1. reading and hearing His Word;
      2. accepting His revelation as God's saving power;

3. engaging in mutual consolation and exhortation; and
4. recognizing each gathering as a further step toward joining the eternal assembly of God's people around His throne.

Lesson 1

The Message of an Apostle
(Overview)

Begin with Devotions

Lay aside the cares of the world by spending some time at the beginning and end of each study session praising our Lord. Just a few minutes of devotion to the Lord can set the mood for study of His Word.

Begin today's devotions by singing "God's Word Is Our Great Heritage." Pray:

Dear Father in heaven, who gave us Your Word to guide us on our way through life, be with us today as we embark on a journey into Your Word. Bless our reading, that we may be enlightened by Your Holy Spirit and learn to live for You in all that we do. In the name of Jesus Christ, Your Son, our Lord. Amen.

Our Goal Today

To help implement the aim of this lesson, ask: **Why do you think it is important to get a general overview of this epistle, which is only 105 verses long?** Point out that individual passages from the Bible are best understood when we are aware of their setting in the whole book under discussion. Use the analogy of a precious jewel put into its own setting to make the point: every passage is a divine jewel, but under the Spirit's guidance, each one has its own particular context.

Introductory Points/The Salutation

Ask the class to read the paragraph under Introductory Points in the Study Guide. Say, **When you write a letter, where do you sign your name? Where do you write the name of the person you're addressing?** Then have the class read the paragraph under The Salutation in the Study Guide. They will no doubt readily identify the three parts of the salutation in the **Acts** and **James** references. In our epistle, A is in **verse 1:** "Peter, an apostle of Jesus Christ"; B includes the rest of **verse 1** and all of **verse 2** except the closing phrase of that verse, which constitutes the greeting.

Ask someone to read **1 Cor. 1:4** and **Eph. 1:3** to observe how a salutation is often followed by a thanksgiving or prayer.

The group may be interested in comparing an example from an ancient secular source. Read (or jot on the chalkboard):

"Antonius Maximus to Sabina his sister, many greetings. Before all things I pray that you are well . . . making mention of you before the gods" (Deissmann, *Light from the Ancient East*, p. 184).

The Author/The Recipients and the Greeting/The Conclusion/The Body

Read and check the references given under these headings.

The Sequence

The class may wish to read in unison the headings for the six major divisions of **1 Peter** as listed in the Study Guide. (Encourage the students to refer to the outline as they study the epistle on their own at home.)

As the leader of the group, you will need to clarify what many Christians somehow fail to grasp, namely, that a virtuous life grows out of God's prior actions that have made us His children. In short, Christian living is a response to God for what He has already done for and to us.

To help you make this point, put on the chalkboard the simple sentence: **Be what you already are!** That is the heart of a God-pleasing life. God has already made us His saints; so now we want to show it! That relationship between God's saving actions and our lifestyle is sharply outlined in the sequence offered as a general outline of the epistle.

If time permits, ask the class to evaluate some approaches to behavior that are commonly heard:

1. "Unless you are good, Jesus (or I) won't love you." (A moralistic and unbiblical approval to any relationship, but especially to that between a parent and a child.) Ask the class to suggest what a biblical approach might be. E.g., "Jesus (and I) still love you, even though what you're doing is wrong. Ask Jesus to help you show you're His child."

2. "If you do the dishes tonight, I'll take you to a movie later." All of us at times use this kind of a tit-for-tat, you-scratch-my-back-and-I'll-scratch-yours approach. But what happens to the relationship when we make our love conditional on the other person's behavior? Again, compare with the approach of this epistle. God's grace is unconditional, *apart from* our works. "We love because He first loved us" **(1 John 4:19)**.

The Occasion

The data given in the Study Guide provide a theory for the occasion of writing **1 Peter.** Many theories exist about what caused Peter to write this epistle, but since he did not state his reason, we can only guess. Have the class read the paragraphs under this heading and check the references cited. Regarding the *Babylon* reference in **5:13:** Point out that the name *Babylon* is used in **Revelation** (e.g., **16:19**) for the city of Rome. According to tradition, Peter resided there for a time and suffered martyrdom there by being crucified upside down. Pitch was then poured over his body, and it was set on fire to help illumine Nero's gardens.

The Destination

This section is best dealt with by consulting a map of the Mediterranean world as it looked in the first century. (Check the back part of your Bible or, if available, use a wall map.) You can trace the route that Silas probably took.

The Purpose

1 Peter 5:12 is so clear on this point that just reading the passage in unison will fix this item in the minds and hearts of each member in the group.

Authority

In this paragraph you will have the opportunity once again to underline the fact that the book under study comes to us with apostolic authority. In this connection, you may want to ask the group, **When you last recited the Nicene Creed, what did you think of when you confessed the church to be** *apostolic?"* The word *apostle* means, literally, "one who is sent." Thus it refers originally to the 12 disciples **(Matt. 10:2)** whom Jesus personally called and sent forth to witness to the Gospel. Peter thus writes as one sent and commissioned by Jesus Christ Himself—He who is Lord of the church. The church is "built on the foundation of the apostles and prophets, with Christ Jesus Himself as the chief cornerstone" **(Eph. 2:20).**

For Group Discussion

1. Invite participants to share their impressions of Peter the person and Peter the child of God as they reflect upon the message of this epistle for their lives.

2. Accept participant responses.

3. Peter wrote to encourage the faithful.

A Glimpse Ahead

Call the group's attention to this last paragraph.

End with Devotions

After singing a hymn such as "Lord, Keep Us Steadfast in Your Word," pray the following prayer:

> Lord Jesus, the Word made flesh, please keep us steadfast in You as we go forth into the sinful world. In everything that we do, let us reflect You. Keep us safe until we meet again to study Your Word. Amen.

Lesson 2
There Is Nothing Like It (1 Peter 1:1–2)

Begin with Devotions

Begin today's study session with a prayer:

> Holy Spirit, be with us today as we study the Word that You revealed to Your saints. Give us an understanding of the text and insight into how it relates to our lives. Amen.

Sing together a hymn such as "The Church's One Foundation."

Our Goal Today

After reading together the goal of this lesson, ask, **Is there anything in the statement of this goal that is new or surprising to you?**

Point out that the word *moved* reminds us that the Scriptures, being the Word of God, are the means by which the Holy Spirit works in our hearts p
75   75 **What images come to your mind at the mention of the word *sanctify*?**

Have the group read together (or individually in various translations) **Rom. 8:29–30**, which is the classic statement on our being chosen (predestined). Point out that this insight into God's action was given us not for the purpose of stirring up all kinds of speculative questions but as a source of comfort. We are asked to trust God for what He did, and we are not to philosophize about all the problems and possibilities connected with our election.

Rom. 8:30 has been called the "parabola of redemption." The movement starts with God's act of predestination before history began. From there the gradient moves down through history, where we live. There God calls and justifies us. At that point the line moves upward into eternity with the verb that tells us that God has already glorified us. You may want to draw such a parabola on the blackboard or prepare it ahead of time on a sheet of paper.

It is essential to keep in mind that the New Testament word *foreknew* does not, primarily, refer to God's knowledge of things before they happen but to His choice by grace before time began.

After this introduction to a key term in today's lesson, ask the members of the group to read aloud the two verses in the various translations of the Bible that may be available. (If possible, bring along a number of different versions yourself to supplement the reading in the group). Compare the different renderings briefly, but stay with the important points.

Origin

Let the group respond to the questions in the first paragraph under this heading. Affirm responses indicating that clubs come in to being by human devises, whereas the church exists because of the work of God. Help the group to see that any local congregation, or assembly of believers, is the manifestation at a particular place of the *ekklesia* (church) as the sum total of all believers of every age and time. (To make that point very clearly and simply you may wish to have a look at **1 Cor. 1:2,** where Paul gives his greetings a local accent while, at the same time, referring to "all those everywhere who call on the name of our Lord Jesus Christ.") Then read the remaining paragraphs under this heading.

Background

Read the paragraphs under this heading in the Study Guide. Then give the class members a little time to research their Old Testament or to recall Old Testament stories that will help them to understand the three key words: *elect, dispersion,* and *strangers.* Let them share their findings. (You may need to get them started in the right direction by mentioning the call of Abraham or Israel's wanderings in the desert.)

In this kind of context you may wish to use the following diagram as a way of orienting yourself and the whole group to the central thrust of Scripture as it applies to a given time:

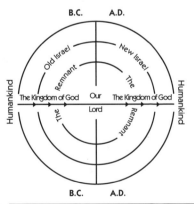

The line moving horizontally through the concentric circles may be called "the Kingdom of God". This is a New Testament expression, which is shorthand for all the bother God went to and still goes to in order to reestablish His rule of grace in and among people. The story begins at the far left with the creation of humankind. God did rule in the hearts and minds of our first parents as they left His creative hand. But they rebelled. The attempt to cleanse the earth at the time of Noah and to begin again with an obedient remnant soon failed. In time, therefore, God chose Israel to be His "kingdom of priests" (Ex. 19:5–6), which is referred to in the diagram at the juncture with the second circle (the remnant). This nation, a community of people, was chosen to serve as the instrument by which God's promises were to be carried forward. At the same time, Israel was called to obedience to serve as a showcase, so to speak, of the blessings God was ready to bestow on those who believed in Him as their Lord.

Not all of Israel remained faithful, however. The next half circle, to the left of the vertical line, represents the obedient remnant, out of which, in due course of time, sprang the One True Israel, Jesus Christ. His coming marks the division in time between B.C. and A.D.

At this point in the illustration the action is reversed. The line moves forward to Jesus' selection of the faithful remnant out of Israel. As there were 12 patriarchs in the story of ancient Israel, so Jesus chose 12 disciples to serve as the core of God's new people. The half-circle to the right of the vertical line corresponds to the one on the left. The Twelve and those who joined their company were baptized by the Spirit on Pentecost Day and so became the church, the new Israel (Acts 2:1–36). To that people—to us!—has been given the task put before Israel of old; namely, to bring the message of God's grace to all people until such time as the Lord returns, which is the point where the horizontal line meets the last half circle on the right.

After sharing this diagram, have the class reconsider the two verses of the salutation and ask, **What new insights do you now have?**

Purpose

Have the class read silently the first half of **Exodus 24.** Then have them share their findings as to what a *covenant* is. Somebody may come up with the thought that it is a contract or deal. Meet such an answer by saying that the word may be used this way in everyday life, but that is not what is meant in **Exodus.** What is described here is a one-way offer from God that was accepted by His people.

In just this way we must think of the term *covenant* whenever we celebrate the Lord's Supper and hear the sentence, "This cup is the new covenant in My blood" (or "this is My blood of the new testament"). What is especially new in this situation is that the relationship we have with God was accomplished and sealed by the blood of none less than God's own Son. In response to that action we, like ancient Israel, are invited to obedience. Among such people God's grace and peace grow and grow in keeping with their needs.

Means

Let individuals in the group first point out some similarities and differences between the church and civic clubs, as suggested in the Study Guide. Then point out that the use of the means of grace is unique to the church. (Emphasize this point if it was not mentioned by the class.)

It is imperative at this point to stress the external nature of what are called the means of grace: Word and Sacraments. Christian congregations almost everywhere are plagued by the practice of a phony kind of piety that has its source in individual experience and feeling. The word applied by Luther to this phenomenon is usually translated with the word *enthusiasm* (*Schwaermerei*). He saw this as a much more serious threat to the Gospel than the teachings of the Roman Catholic Church of his day.

In Article VIII of the Smalcald Articles, for example, the reformer makes the following observation with respect to **2 Peter 1:21:**

> St. Peter says that when the prophets spoke, they did not prophesy by the impulse of man but were moved by the Holy Spirit, yet as holy men of God. But without *the external Word* they were not holy . . .

Allow the class to struggle with the Study Guide question about prayer. Then have the group consider **Matt. 6:5–8.** Again, it is important to reach the point where prayer is seen not as a means of grace but as our response to what God offers us by His grace.

For Group Discussion

1. Accept participant responses. Comment that churches are not only places to receive God's blessings through Word and sacraments, they are also places God's people go to respond to God's goodness to them in Christ.

2. Underscore God's kingdom will endure forever despite persecution and hardship.

3. There is only one church, built on the teachings of the apostles, but founded and rooted in Christ.

4. While there is only one true church, believers organize themselves in congregations and church bodies for purposes of cooperation and fellowship.

A Glimpse Ahead

Read the Study Guide paragraph and **1 Peter 1:3–9.**

End with Devotions

Sing together "Amazing Grace, How Sweet the Sound." Then close with a prayer:

> **Dear Father in Heaven, who sent Your one and only Son to die for us, please forgive us for our many sins. Grant us Your grace and peace in abundance as we go out to live our lives for You. In the name of our Savior, Jesus. Amen.**

Lesson 3

A People with a Place to Go (1 Peter 1:3–9)

Begin with Devotions

Sing a song about Baptism such as "All Who Believe and Are Baptized." Then pray:

> **Holy God, we thank and praise You for Your gift of salvation and for washing us clean in Your waters of Baptism. Be with us today as we remember our baptismal vows. In the name of the Father and of the Son and of the Holy Spirit. Amen.**

You may want to recite together the words of the Apostles' Creed as a way of renewing your baptismal vows.

Our Goal Today

Have the members of the class pick out the key terms in the statement of today's goal in light of the title of this lesson. Then have them read **1 Peter 1:3–9** either in unison or responsively. If additional translations are being used, have individuals read the passage from one or more of these, verse by verse or as a whole.

God Acted in Mercy

Read the paragraphs under this heading in the Study Guide. Then point out that the first form of any kind of creed used in the early church at Baptism was the statement "Jesus is Lord." Ask the class to find an echo of that in **verse 3.** Then ask: **What creed do we use in our baptismal service?** (The Apostles', in which we confess that "Jesus Christ" is "our Lord.")

Baptism: Means of New Birth

Read the Study Guide paragraph. Then ask the class how they understand the expression "born-again Christian." Let them comment on the fact that "born-again people" can often tell you exactly *when* they were "saved," as they put it.

As part of this kind of discussion it is essential to lead the class to the point where they can comprehend the difference between the general use of "born again" as meaning the moment when a person says he or she decided for Christ and Baptism as it is understood in the New Testament.

Point out that it is God's Word that makes Baptism work.

Our Promised Land

Have the group read this section silently. When all or most have finished reading, ask whether there are any questions. Then as one way to demonstrate how devoid of hope the ancient world was, you may wish to ask the class to comment on the following epitaph on the tomb of a contemporary and fellow citizen of St. Paul:

> Here lies Dionysius of Tarsus, sixty years old. He never married and wishes his father had never married either.

You may wish to ask the class to look at some nearby gravestones on their own to find some inscriptions that evidence the Christians' hope in Christ.

In some parts of Christendom it has become a bad practice to reduce the idea of salvation to the single dimension of this present life, making it mean social, political, and economic justice and freedom for everyone. The Bangkok Conference of 1972, called together by the World Council of Churches, did just that. Have your class evaluate such an understanding of "salvation" in light of **verses 4 and 5.** What wording is there, especially in **verse 5,** to preclude limiting God's act of saving to the dimension of this present life alone?

Inquire as to whether the members of your group think of salvation in only other-worldly terms. You may want to introduce them at this point to the word *eschatology.* This church term refers not just to the end of history, when our Lord returns. It is used to speak of the present in light of the end that is sure to come. Have your class look very closely at the end of **verse 5** to formulate their own way of talking about eschatology. As time and interest permit, let class members share their experiences ("already-not yet" question in the Study Guide).

Shielded by God's Power

Read the paragraphs, inviting participants to share answers to the questions.

A Joy That Defies Definition

Read the Study Guide paragraphs and discuss the questions they contain. The apostles rejoiced in their suffering because they had been counted worthy of suffering disgrace for the Name **(Acts 5:41).** Note that Christian joy often puzzles unbelievers. They think that church people live in a kind of dream world, created by a very imaginative kind of faith. What items in the passage under study show that the apostle was a realist?

For Group Discussion

1. Some may define hope as a desire or dream for something better. In the language of this epistle, hope is a confidence in the eternal destiny that is ours by faith in Christ Jesus.

2. The Christian hope is also operative in the here and now. Armed with hope God's people face the challenges and rigors of everyday life in a hostile and alien world.

3. Accept participant responses.

4. Accept responses. Affirm that God always keeps His promises.

Summary

One of the most useful ways of concluding this kind of study is to have each member put down in writing two or three sentences that set forth what new insights he or she has gained from the analysis of the passage studied (in this case, **1 Peter 1:3–9**). Such a challenge can be handled orally, too, and may lead to the matters listed for group discussion.

A Glimpse Ahead

You may point out that **verses 3–9** are part of a larger unit that runs to the end of **verse 12.**

End with Devotions

Celebrate the "inexpressible and glorious joy" of your salvation by singing "Love Divine, All Love Excelling." Then pray:

Lord Jesus Christ, You are love incarnate. We thank You and praise You for humbling Yourself to become human. Lord, You died

for our sins and rose again that we might have eternal life. We can never express the glorious joy we have because of Your actions. Please forgive us for the hurt we have caused You by our sinfulness and give us the strength to live as Your redeemed children in everything that we do. In Your holy name we pray. Amen.

Lesson 4
Our Present Privilege (1 Peter 1:10–12)

Begin with Devotions

Begin with prayer:

Holy God, You alone are worthy of praise. Through Your prophets You foretold the coming of Your Son to be our Savior. Give us Your insight today as we seek to learn more about this wonderful act. We also join together with all the saints and angels to praise You. Amen.

Sing your praises in the song "Holy God, We Praise Your Name."

Our Goal Today

First read together the three verses to be analyzed. Then ask how the statement of the goal reflects what is said in these verses. Does the word *splendor* fit?

Salvation Foretold

Read the first two paragraphs under this heading in the Study Guide. Then ask: **Is it all worthwhile?** Allow ample time for members of the class to express themselves on this point in light of their own experiences and reflections.

Next, let the class members briefly speculate (third paragraph) regarding the kind of questions the prophets might have asked themselves as they looked over their own predictions of the future. Then read and share answers to the questions in the last two paragraphs of this section.

Fuller Dimensions

As you read these paragraphs, you will want to follow through on an examination of the texts indicated in the Study Guide. They deal with the crucial difference between days of old and the age of the Messiah and of His church: the period in which we are now living. Be sure to stress the *now* of **verse 12** and of **Eph. 3:5.**

Proclamation of the Gospel

In this section the text of the Study Guide is self-explanatory, but you will want to take up the matter of Gentiles becoming members of the church. **Acts 15** tells us the story of the storm raised by this issue and how the matter was solved in such a way as to make it possible for non-Jews to become part of the new Israel without having to take up the burden of the many rules and regulations imposed by Judaism. You will want to make a special point of the fact that most, if not all, of the members of your study group are Gentiles, in the Biblical sense of the word, and yet belong to God's very special people, His church. Indicate how, on Pentecost Day, the Spirit was poured out on *all* people **(Acts 2:17)** in keeping with Joel's prophecy. He, too, in his day, must have wondered when his words would be fulfilled!

Angelic Excitement

To the materials given in the Study Guide, which it will be well to read carefully, you may want to add the following item for further reflection by the class. It is from a poem called "The Seraphim."

The poem describes the work of the Son of God on earth as the angels see it. While they watch how things are going—toward the cross, of all things!—one seraph looks at the host of ransomed souls to be gathered up in the church, and then he observes:

> Hereafter shall the blood-bought captives raise
> Their passion-song of blood.

To this another seraph responds by saying,

> And *we* extend
> Our holy, vacant hands toward the Throne,
> Saying, "We have no music!"

Such music is for us to sing. That is why we have hymnals and use them. They are full of *our* music, the songs of the redeemed.

For Group Discussion

1. These verses refer to the unsatisfied curiosity of those who by inspiration wrote of the coming salvation Christ would bring.

2. By the Spirit's power, God's people spoke of the salvation that Christ had won through His life, death, and resurrection.

3. We, too, have come to faith. Futhermore, we desire all others to also come to believe.

A Glimpse Ahead

Have the class note the "therefore" that connects what comes next with what has been covered so far.

Summary/End with Devotions

The most effective way to gather up the thoughts of this particular class session is to have the group sing (or read together) such great poetry as that given by Alexander Pope in the hymn "Rise, Crowned with Light."

Then pray together:

Lord Jesus, You did not come to earth to die and rise again just so we could keep this Good News a secret! Encourage us with Your Word and give us the strength and courage to tell others about You. We remember those who serve You in foreign mission fields, even as we strive to tell others Your Good News here at home. Amen.

Lesson 5

Life as Response to God's Action
(1 Peter 1:13–21)

Begin with Devotions

Have participants list specific blessings from the Lord that they have noticed since you last met. Then sing together "Come, Let Us Join Our Cheerful Songs." Talk to the Lord:

Lord, we come together to worship You. Help our worship be praiseful and worthy. Lord, we come together to learn about You. Bless our learning with insight by Your Holy Spirit and help us apply what we learn to our daily living. Amen.

Our Goal Today

Have the class examine the statement of purpose. Then read the text in various translations to bring out its richness.

The Call for Response

You will want to work through for yourself the materials offered in the Study Guide. Various references are given there. Work through these with the class.

Stress Christian living as a response of God. Alert the class to the difference between setting up certain ethical ideals as matters of achievement and living as persons whom God has declared to be His saints, who are such by means of their contact with God's Word and Sacrament.

You may find it useful to give the class a few moments for quiet reflection on the question, **In what way does my life show that it is one of response to God's actions toward me?** Then ask for a few statements from volunteers. This must be done in the spirit of helpfulness and in such a way as to avoid embarrassing anyone.

You may then, once again, ask what new insights your class has been given into the matter of sanctification. Here you must make sure that everyone understands Christian growth as a way of leaning more and more on God's help. It is not to be thought of as a slowly rising line on a graph. Instead, each day we fall back totally on God's grace by way of contrition and repentance.

One of the most helpful instruments to use in this connection is Luther's answer to the question, "What does such baptizing with water indicate?" He wrote:

> It indicates that the Old Adam in us should by daily contrition and repentance be drowned and die with all sins and evil desires and that a new man should daily emerge and arise to live before God in righteousness and purity forever.

Everyone in the class has probably heard of the practice of zero budgeting: starting over with zero at the beginning of every fiscal year. For Christians this takes place every day. Hence a proper graph for a life in response is *not* the following:

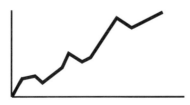

That would suggest our being able to build more and more on our own improved perfection. It would lead us farther and farther away from the bottom line of God's actions and support.

The right kind of graph for Christian living and growth looks like this:

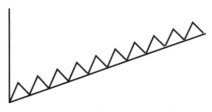

Each day we return to the base line of God's forgiveness and the help of His Spirit.

Draw these two diagrams on a blackboard or a sheet of paper for use in class. To grow spiritually means to learn to depend more and more on God and His grace and less and less on oneself. This kind of progress is well-pleasing to God. Every other kind of growth is self-centered and therefore evil.

Father and Judge

Read orally (or have the group read silently) the paragraphs under this heading in the Study Guide.

Just as God's faithful people believe He will come to judge them, they pray for His help for those He has redeemed with His precious blood. The Christian life consists of responding to God's goodness. Prayer is a vital part of that response. Make it crystal clear that God's act of declaring us to be His saints (justification) is the point of beginning. Sanctification is the life that follows in glad response to God's grace, which is appropriated to us in Baptism.

You ought not to leave this section without making it clear that God's Law, especially as interpreted by the Sermon on the Mount, is our guide in determining what is good in the eyes of God. A good work is what we do in faith according to God's will as expressed by the Ten Commandments, which we call the Moral Law. The Study Guide asks the crucial question of your class members on this matter. You must yourself be very clear on this point: God's Law is not only a kind of mirror to see our sinfulness; it does not just accuse us of our shortcomings. It also offers the only valid guide for our life of sanctification. In addition it is also imperative to remember that the power to live according to the Law comes from the Gospel.

Anyone who keeps God's Law in order to win God's acceptance is only "observing the law" and will go lost unless he repents. But when we follow

God's Law empowered by the Gospel we engage in good works, the kind that are pleasing to God because we stand in the right relationship with Him by having been declared righteous by grace through faith for Christ's sake.

Set Free from Our Own Egypts

Read the paragraphs under this heading. (They introduce the next section.)

Christ, the True Passover Lamb

Discuss the questions in this section of the Study Guide. It is important to help participants understand that what God offers is not "cheap grace." Though God's grace is free to us, it was won at a dear cost—the suffering and death of God's only Son.

For Group Discussion

1. The fruit of the Spirit center on pleasing others rather than on pleasing ourselves.

2. "It is a dreadul thing to fall into the hands of the living God" **(Heb. 10:31).** God is just; He punishes sin.

3. Our righteous actions do not merit us anything in the eyes of our just and perfect God. Only what Christ has done for us and the response He works in us are acceptable to Him.

4. Answers will vary.

A Glimpse Ahead

Encourage the group to keep reading and meditating on this epistle at home.

Summary/End with Devotions

An effective way of "clinching" the points of this study is to have the class read together or sing "Guide Me Ever, Great Redeemer." Or you may ask them to join in saying the Benedictus:

Blessed be the Lord God of Israel, for He has visited and redeemed His people, and has raised up a horn of salvation for us in the house of His servant David, as He spoke by the mouth of His holy prophets, from of old, that we should be saved from our enemies, and from the hand of all who hate us; to perform the mercy promised to our fathers, and to remember His holy covenant, the oath which He swore to our father Abraham, to grant us that we, being delivered from the hand of our enemies, might serve Him

without fear, in holiness and righteousness before Him all the days of our life (Luke 1:68–75 RSV).

Lesson 6
The Church as God's Family (1 Peter 1:22–25)

Begin with Devotions
Begin today's session with prayer:

> O Christ, You are the foundation on which our faith is built. Thank You for establishing Your church here on earth. It is wonderful to worship and learn with other believers! Help us always to remember the purpose of Your church: to tell others about You so that they too may become Your disciples. In Your name, Jesus, we pray. Amen.

Sing together "The Church's One Foundation."

Our Goal Today
You will want to review the general observation from the last lesson that the Christian life is one of response, and then ask how the present statement of purpose moves on from there. Ask the class what it considers to be the key phrase in the sentence. Then have someone read **1 Peter 1:22–25**.

Obedience to Truth
Pursue the questions raised by the Study Guide in the first two paragraphs of this section. The answer to the first question is rather obvious. Regarding the second question, washing one's soul refers to purifying the whole person. To be sure, the word *soul* is occasionally used as a way of calling attention to the fact that people are also *body* and *spirit* (see **1 Thess. 5:23**). Where a distinction is made in Scripture among these three terms, *body* is a way of speaking about people as part of the created visible universe, *soul* relates us to the rest of organic life, and *spirit* is what gives us our unique relationship to God, as described in **Gen. 2:7** (breath of life=spirit). It is our spirit that returns to God at death, according to **Eccl. 12:7**. It was His spirit that Jesus committed into His Father's

hands (**Luke 23:46; John 19:30**). On the other hand, it is the souls of the slain that are referred to in **Rev. 6:9.** This is not the time to go into a detailed discussion of this matter. But you may wish to call attention to this biblical usage very briefly.

To Be God's Family

Read the paragraphs in the Study Guide. Then share this quote from one of the early church fathers: "An individual Christian is no Christian." Ask the class how they react to it in light of the verses under study.

Born Again

Read the Study Guide paragraph. Then explain that our first birth had its source in God's creative power that resides even in perishable seed. Even so, everyone born by way of the biological processes through which God produces life dies. But the seed that is sown from the living and abiding Word of God is imperishable. To be born again means to grow up to eternal life.

Like the Returning Remnant

Let the class read the paragraphs under this heading in the Study Guide. Invite them to share comments on it or questions about it. If time permits, ask the class to look up **Is. 40:6b–8** and to compare these verses with the way Peter gives the quotation. They will discover that one statement from **verse 7** of **Isaiah 40** is missing, and that "our God" in the last line is turned by Peter into "the Lord." In this way Peter emphasizes the baptismal confession that "Jesus is Lord." By confessing the lordship of Jesus Christ, like the faithful remnant returning from Babylon, these newly baptized converts had been made part of a community over which the gates of death cannot ever prevail. Thus it certainly *is* worthwhile to belong to the church!

Just in case anyone would wonder where that Word of the Lord might be heard, Peter makes the point that the Gospel is nothing other than the very message of that lordship of Jesus Christ.

For Group Discussion

1. God would have us demonstrate actions of love to all people—even to our enemies. Through a faithful Christian witness the Good News of salvation in Christ may be shared, and through this message, unbelievers may be brought to faith by the power of the Holy Spirit.

2. The Apostles' Creed summarizes the beliefs and teachings of the faith into which the person is being baptized.

3. Answers may vary.

4. Answers may vary.

Summary

Call attention again to the fact that the church is the body of Christ. Then ask: **What does this mean for the quality of life that we show each other?** Ask the members of the class to write down or to name some specifics. In this connection you may wish to call attention to the fact that the Christian virtues listed, for example, in **Col. 3:12–13** cannot be practiced in isolation. They are relational.

A Glimpse Ahead

A great deal of false teaching has its source in the confusion between goodness and grace. That is what will make a study of the next section **(1 Peter 2:1–8)** rather crucial.

End with Devotions

Rejoice together as members of Christ's church by singing "I Love Your Kingdom, Lord." Then pray:

> **Lord God, earthly kingdoms are built with bricks and stone, mortar and hard work, but Your kingdom is built with Your Word and Your people, Your Son's blood and Your grace. We praise You for Your kingdom and thank You for making us part of it. Amen.**

Lesson 7

The Place of God's Presence in Grace
(1 Peter 2:1–8)

Begin with Devotions

Come together in prayer:

> **Heavenly Father, we crave the pure spiritual milk of Your Word. Help us to grow up in our salvation. Help us to go out and share our salvation with those who have not heard Your Good News. We pray this in the name of Jesus, who is our salvation. Amen.**

Sing together "How Firm a Foundation."

Our Goal Today

The portion of **1 Peter** to be discussed this time is best read in three parts: **verses 1–3; 5–6; 7–8.** You may want to hear each portion read in two or three different translations.

After such a rapid overview, ask the class to pick out two key words in the statement of the goal. (They are *arrangements* and *grace*).

Presence in Grace

Before reading the Study Guide, share this quotation from Luther: "Of course God is present everywhere. He is in water; but we do not drown ourselves to find Him. He is present in the rope; but we do not hang ourselves to locate Him. He is present *for you* in His Word." Point out that some theologians distinguish the two ways of God's presence by calling one the kingdom of His left hand (power) and the other the kingdom of His right hand (grace).

Read the paragraphs under this heading in the Study Guide, checking the parallel Scripture references as you proceed. Help the class to discover references to *the Word* and the *Lord's Supper* in **verses 1–3.** Point out that the NKJV and NET translations ("milk of the word") are better renderings than NIV's "spiritual milk." The apostle here speaks of God's strengthening Word as proper nourishment for newborn (newly baptized) infants. Help the class see that the Lord's Supper is alluded to in **verse 3** by means of a quotation from **Ps. 34:8. Psalm 34** served as the psalm in the Communion service in the congregation in Rome. That is probably the chief reason why that psalm is quoted repeatedly in this epistle (e.g., in **3:10–12**).

A New Kind of Community

Read the first paragraph under this heading in the Study Guide. There may be various guesses by members of the class in answer to the question at the end of the paragraph. Talk about, especially, the role of the pastor during the general and intercessory prayers.

Read the rest of this section. When you reach the reference to **Rom. 12:1,** you will want to have the class devote a few minutes of quiet reflection on the question, "How am I offering myself as a living sacrifice to God?" Unless someone shows some interest in responding to this, it will be best to leave the matter with the individuals in silence.

The Cornerstone

Share the following explanation of *cornerstone:* In the days of the apostle, cornerstones served a purpose quite different from their place in a modern building, where they are merely decorative. They were bondstones put at the corner of the foundation. Centuries ago the cornerstone determined the size and shape of the building. Very often much of the weight of the edifice itself rested in this particular stone. It had to be chosen very carefully, therefore, and given great consideration. That is what God did in planning the spiritual house that would serve Him as a redeemed community. He selected His own Son as the stone that would serve as the very bedrock of the church He proposed to create of those who turn to this divine Son in faith.

The Stone of Stumbling

Read the paragraphs under this heading in the Study Guide. Then share answers to the questions. In the case of the psalmist "the builders" were the Gentiles. They despised God's people as being of no consequence. In fact, many pagans openly ridiculed the people of Israel as not being "with it" because of their belief in and service to a God whom they declared to be the only one. Their enemies served many gods. In this way they became the builders of their own religious rites and their own ethical values.

Jesus used these lines from the psalm to designate the religious leaders of Judaism (Matt. 21:42). They kept stumbling and taking offense at the claims of the prophet from Nazareth. They were "the builders" who rejected the stone put in Zion as the cornerstone of a new kind of temple, consisting of persons who accepted Jesus as the ground and base of their being.

In our present passage "the builders" are all those who try to erect some great edifices of their own. God's chosen cornerstone keeps getting in their way as He points to the vanity of human endeavors undertaken without giving any place or even any thought to the one building stone that really matters. It is their belief that keeps such people from seeing how precious this rock is for their plans and their lives.

What They Were Destined For

Reread verses 7–8 and then the paragraphs under this heading. You must yourself be very sure of what is meant by double predestination. You can also use this discussion to show that it is a basic principle of proper biblical interpretation to understand a difficult passage in light of another very clear passage. 1 Tim. 2:4 is such a clear passage.

For Group Discussion

1. Paul points to those who rely on their own works or righteousness as stumbling over God's gift of salvation. Peter talks about those who stumble as being disobedient. In either case, Jesus—the cornerstone—is rejected.

2. Belonging to Christ is to be part of something solid and enduring yet alive and vibrant.

3. God's Word and faith are the important components of Baptism.

Summary

Since a great deal of mischief is taking place in Christendom today by a failure to distinguish between God's goodness (First Article: kingdom of God's left hand) and His grace (Second Article: kingdom of God's right hand), you will want to return to this distinction. This will provide the opportunity for stressing the two key words in the statement of the goal; for **1 Peter 2:1–8** tells us of the arrangements God has made to be present among us in grace. Close the discussion by having the class reread all eight verses.

A Glimpse Ahead

The church, each congregation, has a job to do. What the major task of the church is will be considered in the next lesson.

End with Devotions

After singing "Christ Is Our Cornerstone," close with a prayer:

Lord Jesus Christ, all around us the world rejects You. Often we also reject You. We ask for Your forgiveness and for Your help as we witness to others about You. Let us build our lives on You, because we know that You are a chosen and precious cornerstone. Amen.

Lesson 8

A People Belonging to God
(1 Peter 2:9–12)

Begin with Devotions

Praise the Lord that He has made you His people by singing "Alleluia! Let Praises Ring." Then pray:

Heavenly Father, the Israelites were in slavery, and You chose them to be Your people. You led them to freedom, You gave them a

new land, and You provided for all their needs. We were in slavery to sin, and You chose us to be Your people. You led us to freedom through the work of Your Son on the cross, You gave us a new land in Your kingdom of believers, and You provide for all our needs, both physical and spiritual. For all this we thank and praise You, ever one God, Father, Son, and Holy Spirit. Amen.

Our Goal Today

Since today's passage comprises only four verses, have one member of the class read all of it. If everyone has the same translation, it may be read in unison.

After reading the passage, have the group pick out the key terms in the statement of the goal. (They are "become more sensitive," "bother" on God's part, "His own.")

Corporate Calling

Read the paragraphs under this Study Guide heading and check the Scripture references outlined there. It will be helpful to recite the First Commandment in unison, as suggested in the Study Guide.

Continuity in Action

Read the paragraphs under this heading in the Study Guide. Then, with the class, explore how the hexagon model fits the life and works of Jesus: (1) Jesus came as an act of God's grace. (2) The first task Jesus undertook in His public ministry was to gather a community of disciples. (3) He was in their midst as the very personal presence of God. In fact, the Greek for "made His dwelling among us" **(John 1:14)** indicates the same presence God had in His tabernacle. (4) Jesus came to obey God's will, saying, "My food is to do the will of Him who sent Me" **(John 4:34).** (5) He also indicated His mission in the familiar statement, "I, when I am lifted up from the earth, will draw all men to Myself" **(John 12:32).** (6) Where His word was rejected, judgment followed, as in the case of Jerusalem itself.

Against this kind of backdrop the apostle Peter used the passage from **Exodus 19** to describe the church as the New Israel, created according to the same pattern: (1) It owes its being to God's grace; (2) it is a community of people that (3) assembles around God's Word and Sacrament, where God is present in His grace; (4) its members are called to obey God's will; (5) their mission is to go out into the world and make disciples of all nations **(Matt. 28:18–20);** and (6) where the proclamation of the Lord's Good News is despised or rejected, people come under divine judgment.

Declare the Praises

Let the class respond to the question. Then supplement (or clarify) what is said with the following points: Baptism is the sacrament that marks the sharp dividing line between darkness and light. Darkness symbolizes sin, death, and damnation—our state before Baptism. Light symbolizes forgiveness, life, and fellowship with God—ours by virtue of Baptism. Its application is God's mighty power of deliverance at work in us. Its fabric is the same as that of the whole series of God's "wonderful deeds": the creation; the choice of Israel; the return of the faithful remnant from the exile; the incarnation, ministry, resurrection, and ascension of Jesus Christ; the creation of the church. (Review the Third Article of the Apostles' Creed.)

Noble Conduct

As time permits, share examples as suggested in the Study Guide. Also, if time permits, explain the phrase "on the day He visits us" **(v. 12)**. Although this phrase may refer to the final day of judgment, it is more likely that the thought expressed here is similar to the one uttered by Jesus in **Luke 19:41–44.** The Lord wept over Jerusalem because He knew of the judgment that would befall this great city. Why? "Because you did not recognize the time of God's coming to you."

It is this visitation of God's grace Peter has in mind. During this period of God's merciful presence, Christians are asked not only to proclaim God's mighty acts but to maintain good conduct, especially by combatting sinful desires. The practice of that kind of lifestyle will move some to glorify God "on the day He visits us," the period of the church's life and work. That is the way in which God's people serve as the light of the world and a city on a hill **(Matt. 5:14).**

For Group Discussion

1. Those who trust in Jesus for salvation need not fear God's judgment. Our debt has been paid by Jesus. We stand before God holy and forgiven through the merits of Christ.

2. Answers will vary.

3. To glorify God in this instance means to repent and come to faith.

4. Participants may refer to the Ten Commandments as they answer this question.

A Glimpse Ahead

Read the preview in the Study Guide.

End with Devotions

Sing together the hymn "Oh, that the Lord Would Guide My Ways." Then pray for that guidance:

Heavenly Father, You have laid out some pretty tough statutes to keep. No matter how hard we try, we stray from Your way. Forgive us, dear Father, and help us keep our eyes focused on You so we may better walk in Your ways. In the name of Jesus, who bought our forgiveness with His holy, precious blood. Amen.

Lesson 9

Attitude toward Government and Economic Systems (1 Peter 2:13–25)

Begin with Devotions

Begin today's session by having participants list some blessings that God has given through our nation. Compile the list and incorporate it into a prayer:

Heavenly Father, You have blessed us with many things, not the least of which is our nation. We know that no matter what country we live in, as long as we live on this sinful earth there will be problems. But we also know that You are a merciful God and have given us and our country many blessings such as [read your list of blessings]. Amen.

Sing together "Before You, Lord, We Bow."

Our Goal Today

Read together the goal as listed in the Study Guide and **verse 13** of the text, which is the topic sentence for this session's study.

In the World but Not of It/The Key Term: Submit

After reading the paragraph under "In the World . . ." let the class share responses to the opening question under "The Key Term . . ." Then proceed with the points made in the rest of that Study Guide section.

To demonstrate the radical difference in lifestyle suggested by the word *submit,* you may use the following two diagrams:

The Ego
Normal Lifestyle
(Centripetal)

The Ego
The New Life
(Centrifugal)

The apostolic call to submission cuts squarely across the path that people normally take. By nature, people set out to exploit others by asserting themselves and their rights. Submission is the reverse of all this. It describes a way of life like that of our Lord's, who never asked, "What's in it for me?" We might call it the *centrifugal* pattern of life, where everything moves away from oneself out towards others. By way of contrast, people normally live according to a *centripetal* pattern; everything moves in toward the center to serve the individual.

Toward Government

Read or have the class read **verses 14–17.** Then continue with the Study Guide commentary. Be sure to discuss the question included in this section. (As citizens of a democracy, we can participate freely in organizations and projects designed to promote human welfare.)

Toward Economic Systems

Have someone read **verses 18–25.** Then read the Study Guide commentary in this section. In handling discussion or questions that may arise from the group, the following points may be helpful: No one ever suffered more unjustly than did our Lord. He was never guilty of the slightest wrong; nor did He use language to deceive anyone. He uttered no threats even while He was being unjustly beaten. Instead, Jesus committed Himself to God as the one who has a way of judging justly. Remembering Him—His forgiveness **(v. 24)** and His trust in the Father **(v. 23)**—enables us to submit ourselves as He did.

Even though we do not live in a slave society, as St. Peter did, the principle expressed in **verses 18–20** still applies. Being able to "submit . . . with all respect" does not mean lying down like a doormat; for, in our kind of open society, citizens are encouraged, even expected, to "sound off" for purposes of helping to determine what kind of arrangements and rules are to be accepted. However, Christians do so from a different motivation:

their major concern is the welfare of others.

For Healing

Have the class reread **verses 24–25** and the paragraphs in the Study Guide. Then ask the members to give an explanation in their own words. Supplement their answers, if needed, by sharing the following: **In both Christ's death and our lives of righteousness there is healing, the kind described in verse 25. Our Shepherd and Overseer is concerned not only for our physical well-being but also for our spiritual wholeness. Instead of frightening isolation and fragmentized individualism, Christians enjoy the community of the church, a sense of continuity with the saints of all ages.**

For Group Discussion

1–3. Accept participant responses. Encourage them to explain their reasoning.

Summary

Emphasize again that the atoning work of Jesus Christ is both the motivation and example as you "submit yourselves for the Lord's sake to every authority instituted among men."

A Glimpse Ahead

Read the sentence in the Study Guide.

End with Devotions

Sing "'Come, Follow Me,' Said Christ, the Lord," then pray:

Lord Jesus Christ, we give ourselves to You. Help us to follow only You in every area of our lives. Help us reflect Your servanthood so that we may be a witness to others. Open our eyes to opportunities of service and make us willing to carry them out. In Your holy name we pray. Amen.

Lesson 10

Life in the Married Estate and in the Church
(1 Peter 3:1–12)

Begin with Devotions

Have the participants share what qualities they would look for when choosing a mate (or, if they are married, what qualities about their spouse attracted them). Apply those traits to the church, the bride of Christ. Do we, as Christians, fulfill those traits? How would the church benefit if we did? Pray:

Lord Jesus, our Bridegroom, forgive us for not loving You as we should. Forgive us for the times we are unfaithful to You. Forgive us for the times we are unkind to others. Please help us to uplift You in all we do. Amen.

Sing together "Love in Christ Is Strong and Living."

Our Goal Today

Point out the three parts of the text for this session: The first six verses present some basic elements of a Christian wife's relationship to her husband. **Verse 7** depicts a Christian husband's responsibilities. **Verses 8–12** describe the new life within a congregation.

Have three different people read each of the three sections. Then read the goal as presented in the Study Guide.

Husbands and Wives

Read and check the references in the first two Study Guide paragraphs under this heading.

In connection with the last paragraph, you may want to share the following: The most notable example in the ancient church of a wife who won her pagan husband over to the Christian faith was Monica, the mother of Saint Augustine. In his *Confessions* (IX:19, 22) her son wrote of her as follows:

So soon as she was of marriageable age, being bestowed upon a husband, she served him as her lord; and did her diligence to win him unto Thee, preaching Thee unto him by her conversation; by which Thou ornament- edst her, making her reverently amiable, and admirable unto her husband . . . Finally, her own husband, towards the very end of his earthly life did she gain unto Thee.

We happen to know about Monica because her son wrote of her. Many other instances could, undoubtedly, be cited if every such case had been noted. Such quiet conversions go on to this very day, many of them unnoticed except by God Himself, which is really all that matters!

Inner Attitude

Read **verse 3** and then pose the question in the Study Guide. Point out that in the case of this verse the general rule applies that a passage must be understood within its context. This is not a blanket condemnation of women who make themselves outwardly beautiful by way of clothing and other adornment. What the apostle condemns is using such items to excess and thereby negating the principle of submissiveness. After all, "outward adornment" can be and often is a means of self-assertion, which is the very opposite of submission.

At the same time, Peter calls attention to the fact that real beauty flows from the inside of a person, comprising, in the case of wives, an "unfading beauty of a gentle and quiet spirit" **(v. 4)**. Gentleness is a quality of the heart ascribed to our Lord Himself on the day He entered Jerusalem riding on a donkey (see **Matt. 21:5**). In God's sight such an attitude is "of great worth," we read. It is seen only in action; otherwise it is a hidden characteristic.

Explore briefly what images are worked in class members' minds by this term *gentleness*. Then point out that gentleness is no "Casper Milktoast" affair. Like quietness, it refuses to take advantage of the other person and so is always ready to yield in consideration of others. Jesus Himself did not come riding into Jerusalem on a white charger after the manner of a conquering hero. He was desperately anxious to win over the inhabitants of Jerusalem, but not in terms of exploitation or self-assertion. He hoped that His fellow Jews might see in His approach the fulfillment of a prophetic utterance and so be won over by a gentleness of spirit that belied every worldly interest.

Have the class read again **verses 5–6.** Then ask a few volunteers to share what they know about Abraham and Sarah. As time permits, share additional observations (in your own words) like these: Sarah is described here as obeying Abraham and calling him "master." As Abraham is the father of those who believe so Sarah is the mother of those who obey. She is here named as the model for Christian wives to imitate. That of itself will add to the kind of inner strength that can put up even with the intimidation of a pagan husband; for such a life consists of doing right. Such doing good of itself is a way of not letting oneself be fearful **(v. 6).**

Fellow Heirs

Have someone read **verse 7.** Then read together the Study Guide paragraphs. Follow up on the question of the radical nature of calling wives fellow heirs of eternal life as a sample of the Good News working as a ferment in society and slowly changing the value systems of whole cultures. In Rome and Greece wives were considered to be chattel. Even an enlightened philosopher like Aristotle could and did say, "It is doubtful that slaves and women have souls."

As time permits, expand on the Study Guide commentary. Point out that, while the words "be submissive" do not occur in this text on husbands, the practical equivalent is here in the exhortation that husbands honor their wives as the weaker partner; for weakness invites assistance. (See also **Eph. 5:21–25.**)

Harmony

Supplement what the class members volunteer in answer to the Study Guide question: To "live in harmony" is no call for stereotypes but an invitation to subsume all tensions and differences under a common loyalty to a single Lord. All the virtues listed in **verses 8–9** are *relational.* No one can practice love or sympathy in a vacuum. Even humility practices the art of ranking oneself below others.

To respond in kind to evil and insult only perpetuates the wrong. "Inherit a blessing" recalls the words of Jesus in the final judgment: "Come, you who are blessed by My Father; take your inheritance" **(Matt. 25:34)**. Peter rounds off his exhortation with a quote from **Psalm 34,** words no doubt familiar to his original readers.

For Group Discussion

1. Accept participant responses.

2. God planned for marriage to be a one flesh union in which partners join together to create a new identify—stronger than either of its two components.

3. Accept participant responses.

4. Humility puts the needs of others ahead of our own as a demonstration of the sacrificial love of Christ at work within us.

Summary

Compare this session's text with the table of duties in **Eph. 5:21–6:9** and **Col. 3:18–4:1.**

A Glimpse Ahead

Encourage participants to return next session to study life under the lordship of Jesus Christ.

End with Devotions

Join hands and sing "Blest Be the Tie That Binds." Keeping your hands joined, pray:

> **Heavenly Father, You have given us the bond of love—Your holy precious love—to join with others. Forgive us for the many times we intentionally break Your bond of love. Give us Your insight by Your Holy Spirit always to see new ways to share Your love with others. In the name of Jesus, who is love. Amen.**

Lesson 11

Life under the Lordship of Jesus Christ
(1 Peter 3:13–22)

Begin with Devotions

Begin the session today by singing "May We Your Precepts, Lord, Fulfill." Then pray together:

> **Lord Jesus, we praise You for Your leadership. Help us always to follow Your example of loving others and serving others so that we may have opportunities to witness about You and Your ultimate servanthood—Your death and resurrection. In all that we do, everywhere we go, let this be our goal. In Your holy name we pray. Amen.**

Our Goal Today

Have someone read **verses 13–17.** Point out that this section has to do with ethics (Christian living). Then have someone read **verses 18–22.** Ask the class to pick out the statements from this section that find an echo in the Second Article of the Apostles' Creed. Then look at the statement of today's goal from the Study Guide. Ask: **What is doctrine in the statement, and what pertains to Christian living?**

Doing Good May Bring on Suffering

Read again **verse 13** and then the first paragraph under this heading in the Study Guide. Then ask: **Why is it that Christian righteousness so often is met with hostility?** Lead the class to see that, since people in general resist God's approach to them, they are annoyed when they see persons who are zealous for what is right. Such devotion troubles their consciences; it shows up the shabbiness and selfishness of their own existence. So they hit back by harassing Christ's followers.

Next, read and comment on **verse 14.** There is an echo here of the Beatitude: "Blessed are those who are persecuted because of righteousness, for theirs is the kingdom of heaven" **(Matt. 5:10).** Christians who suffer for living out their faith have the kingdom of heaven to look forward to; that is no small blessing!

Next, read the remaining paragraphs under this heading in the Study Guide. Share answers to the questions. Encourage the class by reminding them that martyrs of all ages have found strength in these words, including those Christians who today suffer indignities and even tortures in non-Christian countries.

With Gentleness and Respect

Read **verses 16 and 17** and the Study Guide paragraphs.

The question about Stephen will give you a chance to point out that in the church year his day of martyrdom follows on the very day after Christmas. That is a way of reminding church people of the cost of discipleship!

Our Model and Warrantor

Read **verses 18–19** and then the commentary and questions in the Study Guide. Next, read **verse 20,** which tells us who the spirits were to whom Christ preached. In Jewish thought Noah's generation was the most lost of all generations; for they had heard Noah, the preacher of righteousness **(2 Peter 2:5)** and had rejected his message. These departed spirits occupied the most abandoned level of hell. To that place the risen Christ went to proclaim Himself Lord also of that region. The simple word *preached* means that Jesus Christ announced His victory over death and hell. For those who had not believed Noah this was very bad news indeed!

During the long centuries of the church's history, individuals, including renowned theologians, have done a great deal of speculating about all that might have happened in hell when the Messiah descended there. They have written long and detailed descriptions on the subject of the harrowing of hell: devils scattering in all directions at the approach of the Son of God in His power. Some parts of the church have taught that Christ went there to liberate the saints of old from their limbo, as it was called. There is nothing in the passage before us along those lines.

Flood-Baptism

Read **verses 20–21** and then the first paragraph under this heading in the Study Guide. Point out that the person to be baptized is asked, "Do you renounce the devil and all his works and all his ways?" The response is in the form of a *pledge*.

In connection with the last Study Guide question, comment that **verse 22** means that Jesus' rule extends from the nethermost regions of hell to the farthest reaches of heaven. Jesus Christ is literally "King of kings and Lord of lords."

Through Baptism God in Christ offers forgiveness of sins, rescues from death and the devil, and gives eternal salvation to all who believe this, as the words and promises of God declare.

For Group Discussion

1. Accept participant responses.
2. God is truly present in the Sacrament of the Altar.

Summary

The best way to conclude and summarize this lesson is to join in the words of the Third Article of the Nicene Creed.

A Glimpse Ahead

Next time we shall take up all of chapter 4 and consider the subject of the church as a suffering and serving community.

End with Devotions

Because Baptism is such a special event in each person's life, have the participants share what they know about their Baptisms. If they were baptized as infants, perhaps they have heard stories about it from relatives. If they were baptized as older children or adults, they may remember the event themselves. At the very least, encourage them to find out the date of their Baptisms and celebrate with their families and friends on that special day each year. Celebrate now by singing "Baptized into Your Name Most Holy." Then pray together:

> **Dear Father, Son, and Holy Spirit, into whose name we were baptized, thank You for washing us clean from all our sins. Help us daily to remember our baptismal vows and to live as Your redeemed children, serving You in all we do. Amen.**

Renew together your baptismal vows by reciting together the words of the Apostles' Creed.

Lesson 12

A Suffering and a Serving Community
(1 Peter 4:1–19)

Begin with Devotions

Begin today's session by singing "God of Grace and God of Glory." Then pray:

> **Glorious God, You alone are worthy of our praise. You keep us in Your guidance every day as we live our lives for You. Sometimes the hardest thing for us to do for You is to tell others about Your marvelous deeds—especially that of sending Jesus to die and rise again for us. Give us wisdom and courage to speak out this wonderful news, and also to know how best to serve You and others. In the name of Jesus, our Savior and Redeemer, we pray. Amen.**

Our Goal Today

Read the goal as given in the Study Guide.

Baptism: End of Chapter One

Read and follow the directions in the Study Guide. In regard to the first paragraph, emphasize again how Christian values have changed the outlook of whole societies. Our own culture, corrupt as it is, has been affected by the work of the church; and so raw vices are not practiced quite so openly. Furthermore, even many non-Christians today frown on the kind of immoral acts and godless utterances that are also part of life around us.

The prospect of a just judgment **(v. 5)** has always been a source of strength for Christians in their sufferings. That is one reason for their being ready, like their Lord in His ugly experiences with scoffers, to entrust their care to the one who judges justly **(2:23)**.

Pressures of the End Time

Read and follow the directions in the Study Guide. You may want to supplement the reference to hospitality by sharing the following: There was a much greater need for the practice of keeping open house for fellow Christians in those days than now; for Christians at times had to move in order to escape local harassment. Wherever they went, they could expect to find the homes of fellow believers open to them.

Suffering with Christ

Read **verses 12–19.** Then let the class respond to the two questions in the Study Guide.

There are many instances in Scripture of God's people undergoing painful trials, not the least of which is that of our Savior's suffering. The RSV translates this phrase as a "fiery ordeal," which brings to mind the experience of the three men in the fiery furnace as told in **Daniel 3**. This motif of three young men surrounded by flames of fire occurs repeatedly among the paintings still to be seen in the catacombs at Rome, where early Christians worshipped. We can conclude from that fact to what extent this story of the fiery furnace proved to be a source of comfort amid the trials and tribulations of those early martyrs.

Regarding **verse 17,** you may wish to comment that this observation always sounds strange to ears accustomed to thinking of discipleship as a way of escaping suffering or judgment. Peter looks at this subject in just the way the prophet Amos did (**Amos 3:2**).

Peter wrote **verses 17–18** as a source of comfort for his readers. At the same time, this was a reminder that God is indeed holy, and that every transgression—especially the sin of His own people—is an offense that deserves to be condemned by bringing on suffering. However, whatever it is that the righteous experience is just the beginning, a small portion, of the judgment that will overtake the impious and sinful.

For Group Discussion

1. Those who have been baptized into Christ are equipped to dedicate their entire lives to Him, seeking the will of God and avoiding sin.

2. Accept participant responses.

3. God in Christ gives believers the power of His Holy Spirit so that we may endure suffering for the sake of the cross willingly, patiently, and confidently just as Christ endured it for us.

4. The persecutions Christians endure serve to purify God's people. God will continue to work good through suffering for those who belong to Him (**Rom. 8:28**).

Summary

Let the class react to these words by Christopher Dawson: "Every crisis is a rehearsal for the real thing: God's final judgment!" (Point out that the word *crisis* really means "judgment." Christian suffering, therefore, is further witness that the end of all things is at hand!)

A Glimpse Ahead

Next session concludes the study under the theme of the church as God's flock.

End with Devotions

If participants feel comfortable doing so, have them share crisis events of their lives. Especially focus on how God worked good from each crisis. If they are unable to see any good in the situations, brainstorm together to come up with ideas. (Perhaps a hospital stay allowed you to meet new people to whom you could witness. Perhaps the prolonged illness of a loved one strengthened your prayer life.) Pray together:

Lord Jesus Christ, You have promised that Your power is made perfect in weakness. Lord, we come before You as weak people, often frustrated and overwhelmed by the trials of life. Forgive us for trying to solve all our problems by ourselves. Help us to always turn to You for help and strength. In Your name we pray. Amen.

Close by singing "In You Is Gladness."

Lesson 13
We Are God's Flock (1 Peter 5:1–14)

Begin with Devotions

Since part of today's lesson talks about Jesus as our Chief Shepherd, begin today's session by reading together **Psalm 23.** Or sing together "The Lord's My Shepherd, I'll Not Want." Then pray:

Dear Shepherd, sometimes we, Your sheep, wander away and You have to bring us back to You. Forgive us for our wanderings; thank You for calling us back; help us to be faithful members of Your flock. Amen.

Our Goal Today

Ask the class to identify the two key terms in the statement of today's goal (*virtues* and *flock*).

Shepherding God's Flock

Ask a volunteer to read the first four verses. Then ask another volunteer to read the Study Guide paragraphs. Follow up with the two questions in the Guide.

The art of shepherding is not well known among us. We live in a very different type of culture from the one in which Simon Peter grew up. In his day the picture of a shepherd leading a flock and protecting it against beasts of prey was a rather common one. Hence the Bible abounds in the use of language associated with the work of such men as heard the angels sing on Christmas Eve.

The most popular of psalms begins with the line, "The Lord is my shepherd." The word is used of God as the King of His people. Ancient kings and prophets were often referred to as shepherds. They had the job of gathering the scattered, providing the means of sustaining people, leading and guiding them, not to mention their responsibility of guarding the persons entrusted to their care against every kind of danger.

A pastor models what his members ought to be when he himself lives in a humble, non-domineering relationship with his flock (**v. 5**).

The Art of Humility

Reread **verse 5** and then read also **verses 6–7**. Then read the commentary in the Study Guide under this heading. As the Study Guide suggests, let class members recall for one another the events of the first Maundy Thursday.

Danger All Around

Read **verses 8–11** and then the first paragraph under this heading in the Study Guide. Recall the occasion when Peter denied his Lord (**Luke 22:54–62**). Point out just how easily Simon was taken in by the devil.

Remind the class of the familiar lines from "A Mighty Fortress Is Our God": "Deep guile and great might / Are his dread arms in fight." But also recall the other lines: "The Word they still shall let remain / Nor any thanks have for it; / He's by our side upon the plain / With His good gifts and spirit." Then read the remaining Study Guide paragraphs in this section.

Glory

Read the Study Guide paragraphs.

Conclusion

Read the first paragraph in the Study Guide.

Peter uses his concluding remarks to add his own personal exhortation and testimony to what has been said in the letter in terms of "the true grace of God." In his greetings he includes the church in Rome, here referred to by the words, "She who is in Babylon." Like his readers, she too has been "chosen"—a word that takes us all the way back once more to the salutation, where all the readers of this letter are so addressed!

The reference in the Study Guide to extending the peace with a handshake may provide the occasion to discuss the merits of this practice.

For Group Discussion

1. Help participants relate the acceptability of kissing as a social greeting according to the stardards of the culture in wich members of the church live and function. The point here is that God's people greet and relate to one another in ways that signify and relate the love of Christ.

2. Accept other names for the devil, including Satan, evil one, adversary, Beelzebub, prince of devils and demons, and ruler of this world.

3. The twofold purpose of the letter, as alluded to in the Study Guide question, may be paraphrased as follows: Peter wrote this letter to encourage his hearers and to testify to the grace of God.

Summary/End with Devotions

Sing "A Mighty Fortress Is Our God" as a fitting summary of the lesson and the course. Then conclude with prayer:

> Dear heavenly Father, as we go forth into this sinful world, help us always to keep our eyes focused on You so that we can avoid the temptations of the Evil One. Let us live as witnesses of Your might and holiness. In the name of Jesus, our Savior, we pray. Amen.

Real lives facing real frustrations need Connections to God and to one another.

The **Connections** Bible study series helps take the concerns of our heart and turn them over to Jesus in worship, prayer, Bible study and discussion.

Connections uses a Gospel-centered message to build trust in God and to develop trusting and supportive relationships with one another, just as Christ intended.

Connections studies look at small portions of Scripture that really hit home, in areas where anxiety is often deepest.

For small groups or individual study, **Connections** uses God's Word to build relationships and bring peace to troubled hearts.

Ask for **Connections** at your Christian bookstore.

Find Heali *ian Support Studie*
for Individua
or Group

THE
M
7

J esu

and

pos

weighin

and sh

will le

maturi

ences,

who fac

Behavior
Divorce
tility
Abuse

Copir